WHOLE WHEAT BREADMAKING

SECRETS

OF THE

MASTERS

MADE EASY

A STEP BY STEP METHOD BOOK

Whole Wheat BreadMaking

Secrets of the Masters Made Easy

A Step by Step Method Book

By Diana Ballard

This book is not intended for individual medical advice. Persons with medical conditions or who are taking medication should discuss any diet and life-style changes with their health professional.

First Printing August 1993
Second Printing February 1994
K24C

ISBN: 1-55517-120-6
Library of Congress Catalog Card Number: 93-72500
Published and distributed by:

CFI
Cedar Fort, Incorporate
925 North Main, Springville, UT 84663 801-489-4084

Cover Design by Lyle Mortimer
Typeset by Brian Carter
Lithographed in the United States of America

MAMA'S BREAD

I left my potato in the coals
because even Tommy laughed at me
for losing at Kick-The-Can,
so I scuffed my way home from the bonfire
    hungry.

A whiff of wood-burning heat,
fragrance of hot bread
billowed through the doorway.

Surprised by any good thing that night,
I watched Mama take a loaf from the oven,
break open its ruddy brown crust.

Fierce aroma,
walnuts and hot honey
breathed through the room
with all the tenderness
Mama had folded into the dough.

Apricot butter
drenched my handful of bread
and dripped through my fingers,
which could not hold
all the healing.

—*Doris Ida Black*

Written by my mother, who shared these memories and gave me my own.

TABLE OF CONTENTS

INTRODUCTION

Have you ever made a loaf of whole wheat bread and it turned out as heavy as a brick?

Or have you ever tried to slice your beautiful loaf of homemade wheat bread, only to have each slice crumble into a thousand little pieces?

I too, have made my share of wheat flour bricks, and I have made plenty of wheat crumble instead of wheat bread.

Many of us have made white bread with some success, yet when we try to make whole wheat bread, we sometimes fail miserably. Be consoled that whole wheat flour contains 30% more components than white flour. With a little knowledge and practice, we can learn to work with those extra compo-nents, and successfully master the art of whole wheat breadmaking.

The rewards of breadmaking with whole wheat flour are many. The smell and taste of hot bread in Mother's kitchen is such a sweet remembrance. Don't we all relish the peace, security, and good-ness that comes from such memories? As you develop your breadmaking skills, you'll also be providing these mem-ories for the significant people in your life. If your bread is made with 100% whole-grain flour, it is also one of the most nutritious foods known. Two hundred years ago, Benjamin Franklin stated,

"The doctor of the future will give no medicine, but will interest his patient in the care of the human frame, in diet and in the cause and prevention of disease."

We now live in that future spoken of by Ben Franklin. Medical scientists are now telling us that a diet based on whole grains, legumes, fruits, and vegetables can help prevent many of the major diseases. 100% whole wheat bread has an abundance of nutrients that are critical to good health and disease prevention. As an added bonus, wheat bread costs very little to make (only about $.18 for an average loaf).

There are many good recipes to choose from in making whole wheat bread. Some recipes call for very basic ingredients (flour, water, yeast, salt, sugar, and oil). Some recipes call for a greater variety of ingredients (all the above, plus honey, molasses, lecithin, dry milk, gluten flour, eggs, etc.)

The principles of good breadmaking are a constant. If you learn these principles, you can vary the ingredients in the bread and still get excellent results. Experience is by far the best teacher when making bread. Be persistent with your breadmaking until you achieve the results you want!

BEFORE YOU BEGIN

Before you make your first batch of whole wheat bread, be sure to read through the breadmaking concepts and instructions at least twice. The first time will acquaint you with the principles of whole wheat breadmaking. The second time will solidify the concepts in your mind, making your breadmaking more successful.

This book is organized into four large chapters. The first chapter goes into detail about each ingredient in wheat bread. It also discusses why and how wheat bread is made the way it is. The second chapter includes recipes and instructions for making basic wheat bread. It includes options for changing the ingredients in the recipes, creating a wide variety of recipes to use. The third chapter contains more bread recipes. Only enough detail is given to make each recipe. The fourth chapter will help you solve your breadmaking problems.

Once you become an experienced breadmaker, you will probably only need to use part of the second chapter and the third chapter, where the recipes are located.

Also, there are kitchen machines that mix and knead bread dough automatically. The dough is then removed to another container, either a bowl or bread pans. I refer to this type machine as a breadmixer.

Another type of machine is an automated bread machine that mixes the dough, allows it to rise, then bakes it. Such a machine will only bake one loaf of bread at a time. I refer to one of these machines as a breadmaker.

Chapter One

Learning the Basics

Nutrients In Wheat

Wheat, also known as the "staff of life," is literally that! More than a third of the world's population receives more than half of their daily caloric needs from wheat. Wheat is the most nutritious of all the grains, being especially rich in B vitamins and proteins.

A wheat kernel is divided into three main parts; the outer layer, called the bran; the inner starchy layer, called the endosperm; and the tiny embryo at the base of the kernel, called the germ.

The outer layer, or the bran layer, makes up 14% of the wheat kernel, and is removed when making white flour. Most of the B vitamins in wheat are contained in the bran layer (although there is still plenty of B complex in the endosperm and germ as well).

B vitamins are known to strengthen the nerves. If stress is a part of your life, you can really help yourself by including whole wheat in your diet. Wheat bran also contains protein, Vitamins A, C, and E, biotin, folic acid, inositol, chlorine, calcium, cobalt, choline, copper, iron, fluorine, iodine, magnesium, manganese, phosphorous, potassium, silicon, sodium, sulfur, zinc, and other trace minerals.

Health experts are now telling us that we need more high-fiber foods in our diets. Wheat bran is not only rich in vitamins and minerals, but is the single best food source of dietary fiber. In highly industrialized countries, food is generally more refined than in less developed countries. Interestingly, colon cancer is the second leading cancer-caused death in North America. Yet in Third World countries, were two and one-half times the fiber is consumed, only occasionally does one find a death caused by colon cancer. High fiber diets have also been linked with low rates of heart disease, constipation, gallstones, diabetes, hemorrhoids, and systemic cancer.

The endosperm layer of the wheat kernel is the starchy layer. It contains about 83% of the wheat protein, and is the source of white flour.

Wheat germ is the life of the wheat kernel. It contains all the nutrients needed to start new wheat growth, although it represents only 3% of the kernel. Wheat germ is rich in B vitamins, Iron, potassium, magnesium, zinc, and protein. Wheat germ also contains wheat germ oil, which is a good source of natural Vitamin E.

Wheat flour is one of the least expensive sources of high quality protein (approximately $.15 per pound). When compared with animal protein at $2.00 per pound, Wheat flour is indeed a bargain.

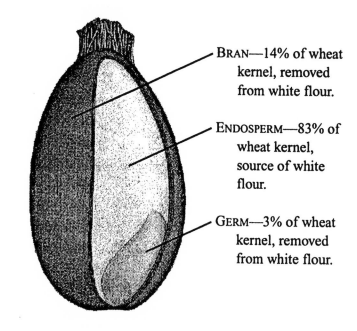

BRAN—14% of wheat kernel, removed from white flour.

ENDOSPERM—83% of wheat kernel, source of white flour.

GERM—3% of wheat kernel, removed from white flour.

(Courtesy of Lehi Roller Mills Co., Inc.)

EQUIPMENT

KITCHEN TOOLS

Following is a list of basic kitchen tools that will help ensure your success:

- Liquid Measuring Cups
- Dry Ingredient Measuring Cups
- Measuring Spoons
- Spatula
- Large Bowl for mixing and/or rising
- Small Bowl for softening yeast (if you use regular, non-instant yeast)
- Bread Thermometer for correct water temperature
- Rubber Scraper to clean dough from bowl
- Kitchen Scale to weigh dough if desired
- Small Ruler to measure rising dough
- Rolling Pin if desired to form loaves
- Pastry Brushes to brush shortening on pans, or to brush tops of loaves with milk or butter

- Thin Cloths to dampen and cover rising loaves
- Muffin Tins, baking sheets, 8 or 9 inch round or square pans for baking fancy rolls and breads
- Cooling Racks
- Spray-on Cooking Oil for bread pans
- Standard Size baking pans (7 1/2 inches long, 3 1/2 inches wide on bottom, 2 3/4 inches deep)

Be sure to use a standard size pan, as given above, because of the width of the pan. It is difficult to have success with wheat bread in wider bread pans. However, deeper pans seem to work even better than the standard depth. Unfortunately, these are only available to commercial bakers. The deeper pan helps prevent bread dough from falling over the sides of the pan while baking. You may be able to locate a commercial type bread pan, and if so, take the opportunity to try it out. You may really like the

results. The small baby loaf pans (one cup dough) are very easy to use, and give variety to the size of your loaves.

I have personally found great success with cast iron bread pans. Cast iron cookware is well known for its even heat distribution and maintenance.

One hundred years ago, Great-Grandma was probably ecstatic to put away her heavy cast iron bread pans in favor of new, lighter aluminum pans. Her bread was probably still great, because she was still cooking in her cast iron stove. Not until the invention of gas and electric stoves did anyone begin to notice that bread was baking unevenly.

Since I have begun using cast iron bread pans, I have yet to experience oddly shaped loaves coming out of the oven. I have loved being able to count on those pans to give me even heat.

Cast iron bread pans may be found at camping and sporting equipment stores.

I have baked bread in many different ovens, most of which heat unevenly. The center of any oven has the most even heat, but we use all of our ovens, not just the center. So how can an oven be made to bake evenly?

The ideal is a convection oven that circulates hot air through the oven, and keeps the heat evenly distributed. These ovens are quite a bit more expensive than conventional ovens. Hopefully, as kitchen technology advances, convection-type ovens will become less expensive.

If you are one of the many cooks who do not have a convection oven, there are other alternatives. Many kitchen specialty shops carry special tiles or rocks that can be placed in the oven to help even out the heat. This partially simulates a brick oven. Brick ovens have for centuries provided steamy, even heat for baking bread. Famous breads around the world are still baked in brick ovens.

Be willing to experiment a little with bread pans, and become familiar with how your oven heats. It could make a big difference in your finished loaves.

Electric Mills

Because wheat contains so much life-giving nutrition, you may want to consider purchasing your own wheat mill. By milling flour immediately before its use, you capture 100% of the nutrients in the wheat.

I'd like to share with you the experience I had in my search for a good wheat mill. It may help you as you decide which mill to purchase.

In 1978, I decided to purchase a wheat mill. Until that time I had been using a little hand grinder, which left my wheat flour quite coarse. For years, I heard that stone-ground flour was the best wheat flour available. I was delighted to finally find an electric "stone" mill, and I was convinced it was the ultimate milling machine. So, I purchased it, took it home, and used it. However, it milled the flour quite hot and was very slow.

I learned a few years later that the stones (hard sandstones) for the original stone grinding mills were quarried especially for their hardness and porosity. However, because few of these stones were still available, the stones in my mill (and most other stone mills for home use) were made of aluminum oxide, or silicon carbide.[1] I knew that the stones were gradually wearing out, but when I realized that they were wearing out into my flour, I began looking for another mill.

Then I found a new mill that used two stainless steel grinding surfaces to mill the wheat. I was very pleased with the mill, because I no longer had to worry that my family was eating residue from aluminum or silicon stones. Because it had stainless steel grinding surfaces, it was also very effective in milling moist or oily grains (rice, peanuts, corn, etc.)

Unfortunately, the milling process was hot (165 degrees F.) like the stone mill. The heat from milling was damaging the gluten in my flour (gluten is the elastic framework that develops during the kneading process, holding the bread together). My bread was always crumbly. The mill was also so slow that I would have to take one afternoon to mill my wheat, then save the flour until another day to make bread.

Soon after, I was introduced to a mill that shattered the wheat kernels against steel teeth, instead of rubbing or grinding them between stones or plates. The resulting flour was fine, and also cool enough that the gluten was not damaged. The mill was also very fast. I now use this type of mill and have been very pleased with it.

You may find an electric wheat mill that operates differently than any of the mills described above. Whether a mill is fast or slow, it should be able to mill wheat into fine flour without getting much above 135 degrees F. You can also judge how well a mill will perform by reading the warranty. It will reflect exactly what the mill is capable of doing.

If your hearing is sensitive, listen to several mills in operation. Be sure to find a mill that has a tolerable noise level. Otherwise, you may need to find high quality ear protection.

To find home wheat mills, check in kitchen gourmet shops, specialty food outlets, grain outlets, or country living catalogs.

HAND MILLS

Hand wheat mills take longer to use than electric mills, but do not require electricity. They are slower than electric mills and wear out more rapidly. Even so, a hand mill is especially good to have on hand in the event of a power failure. Hand milled flour needs to be very fine if it is going to be used for bread. If you do purchase a hand mill for yourself, make sure that it mills flour very fine. If it has stones, make sure that the stones are not made with any type of aluminum. It could have an adverse effect on your health. Take some time to look for a mill that will last a long time, and will serve you with the least amount of work on your part!

BREAD MIXERS

I believe that everyone should learn to make whole wheat bread by hand before purchasing a bread mixer. The experience is invaluable. However, whether or not you have made bread by hand, a bread mixer is a great tool to have in the kitchen. Once you've decided to go looking for a bread mixer, there are a few tips that may help you in making your choice.

Make certain that the machine is made with as many safety features as possible. Make sure, as with the wheat mill, that the noise level is tolerable for you. Because wheat bread dough is so heavy, look for a bread mixer that has at least 500 watts of power. Anything less may not adequately knead your dough. Make certain that the machine has been made well and will last a long time (check the warranty). Make sure that the machine has the proper capacity for your needs. If you need four loaves each time you make bread, don't

settle for a machine that makes only two loaves.

If the bread machine has other functions (food processing, blending, etc.) make certain that the parts are easy to assemble, use, take apart, and clean. Otherwise the machine may end up gathering dust.

Take enough time when looking for a wheat mill or bread mixer to find exactly what you want. These could become the most frequently used appliances in your kitchen.

Automatic Breadmakers

An automatic breadmaker that makes really good whole wheat bread is great to have in any household. I chose to test only three of the many breadmakers on the market. The Zojirushi Model BBCC-S15 is the only Breadmaker that can be programmed to knead, rise, and bake shorter, or longer, as desired. When making 100% whole wheat bread, these options can make a big difference in the finished product. I also tested the Panasonic Model SE-BT65P because it features a whole wheat bread cycle. This cycle is not programmable, but does address some of the special challenges of making whole wheat bread. I also tested the Hitachi Model HB-B101, not because of its specific ability to make whole wheat bread, but its reliability and its excellent representation of breadmakers in general.

I was pleased with the performance of all the breadmakers I tested. Whether you are considering one of the above mentioned machines, or a completely different breadmaker, make certain that the machine you purchase is a quality machine. Your whole wheat bread will only be as good as the machine that makes it. Once you understand the principles of breadmaking, you should have success as you use and enjoy your breadmaker.

Buying, Milling and Storing Wheat

Buying Wheat

If you choose to buy wheat and mill it yourself, make sure that the wheat you purchase is either hard white spring wheat or hard red winter or spring wheat. All types of wheat are high in fiber, and may cause digestive difficulty until you are accustomed to using wheat in your diet. If you are able to eat whole wheat products with no difficulty, it probably will not matter whether you use hard red or hard white wheat. However, if you have continuing digestive difficulty when you use hard red wheat, you may want to try hard white wheat. It seems to be easier on the digestive system than the red wheat because of its slightly different chemical makeup.

The wheat you purchase should also be high in protein (16-20%). There are soft wheats available, producing what is called whole wheat pastry flour, but they are lower in protein (6-10%) and do not make good bread (although they do make good cakes and cookies).

After you have found a high-protein wheat, check to see if it is labeled "Baker's Quality." There are six different proteins in wheat. Only two of these proteins will develop into gluten. These two proteins (called gliadin and glutenin) need to make up a high percentage of the proteins in the wheat. Otherwise, your bread will not develop gluten.

Baker's Quality wheat has been tested to make certain that the two necessary breadmaking proteins are contained in the wheat.

If you find a hard variety of wheat that is very high in protein, but the label does not indicate Baker's Quality, it may still contain the two necessary proteins for breadmaking. Buy a small amount, go home and make bread with it. You will then know whether or not to buy it in bulk.

The type of hard wheat you select for use in breadmaking is probably the single most important factor in your degree of success! If the breadmaking proteins are low (11-15%), success will be more difficult than if the breadmaking proteins are high (16-20%).

It is well worth the time to find the wheat that will work the best for you.

Following are a few sources for wheat. If none of these are accessible to you, check with your local health food stores, or kitchen specialty shops for the best source of wheat in your area.

Wheat Montana Farms
P.O. Box 647
Three Forks, MT 59752
1-800-535-2798

Arrowhead Mills, Inc.
P.O. Box 1866
Hereford, TX 79045

Walnut Acres
Penns Creek, PA 17862

Lehi Roller Mills
East Main Street
Lehi, UT 84043

Erewhon Trading Co.
33 Farnsworth St.,
Boston, MA 02210

Honeyville Grain Inc.
1756 S. 4250 W.
Salt Lake City, UT 84104
(801) 972-2168

MILLING WHEAT

After purchasing your wheat, you will want to mill it and make bread with it. Wheat needs to be milled fine enough to allow the gluten framework to develop during the kneading process. If the wheat is too coarsely ground, the gluten cannot be developed. Most electric wheat mills for home use are designed so that the finest mill setting is used to make very fine pastry flour. Breadmaking flour does not need to be quite that fine, so use the next setting for bread flour.

If you are using a hand mill for your wheat, you will probably have to mill the flour on the finest setting. Depending on your mill, you may have to mill the flour a second time to get it fine enough for bread. You will know that your flour is too coarse for breadmaking if it is the texture of uncooked germade, or Cream of Wheat™. You may want to buy a small amount of whole wheat flour at the grocery store, and compare it with your home milled flour, just to make sure you have the right texture setting on your mill.

If your mill gets hot (140 degrees F. or higher) when it has to grind fine, the gluten may be damaged from the high milling temperature. If your flour seems hot after it is milled, use your kitchen thermometer to check the temperature of the flour. You may choose to leave your flour a little on the coarse side in order to keep your milling temperature down around 135 degrees F.

When milling wheat into flour, one cup of grain yields almost one and one-half cups of flour. For example, if your recipe calls for three cups of flour, mill only about two and a fourth cups of wheat.

STORING WHEAT

You may decide to purchase hard wheat in bulk so that you have plenty on hand for bread-making. If you do, make certain that the moisture content of your wheat is no higher than 10%.

Make certain that your wheat is very clean. Wheat generally will not be troubled by weevil if it is thoroughly cleaned before marketing. Compare the wheat from several outlets before you purchase it in bulk. Not only will you avoid having weevil in your wheat, but also small rocks or other foreign matter that can damage your wheat mill.

Wheat is generally sold in large paper transport bags. After you purchase wheat, it is best to repackage it either in metal cans, plastic buckets with rubber seals in the lids, or glass containers. If humidity is a problem in your location, it is a good idea to locate a cannery that will help you can your wheat for storage in sealed metal cans. If desired, small-scale canning equipment can be purchased or rented for home use.

Wheat will keep indefinitely with nutrients intact if stored properly, away from insects, moisture, and excessive heat.

Several old wive's tales circulate about wheat storage. One of them is that bay leaf or mint will keep weevil out. As was mentioned earlier, clean wheat is the best deterrent to weevil. However, insects may be killed by freezing wheat for 7-14 days at 0 degrees Fahrenheit.

There are two schools of thought on the use of dry ice to kill weevil or to seal cans of wheat. One belief is that an atmosphere of carbon dioxide will destroy weevil—and this has proven to be true.

About one-fourth pound of dry ice is placed on top of two gallons of wheat in a bucket. The remainder of the bucket is filled with wheat and the lid is loosely placed on the bucket for six hours. It is then sealed tightly so that there is an oxygen-deprived atmosphere inside the bucket for seven to ten days. This kills any weevil and eggs.

The other school of thought is that although dry ice provides an oxygen-deprived environment, it also introduces moisture into its environment as it evaporates. In a warm, humid climate, this can definitely shorten the storage life of your wheat. It may well be that wheat, in warm, damp climates, is best stored in sealed cans.

If you want to eliminate the chance of having any weevil in your wheat, you can put it in a freezer at zero degrees Fahrenheit for two weeks. This kills any weevil and their eggs. This works for flour as well.

If weevil do get in your wheat or flour simply use a screen to clean it. If the infestation is heavy you may choose to replace the wheat or flour with new product.

BASIC BREAD INGREDIENTS

WHOLE WHEAT FLOUR

The most basic ingredient in wheat bread is 100% whole wheat flour, milled from high protein, low moisture wheat.

If you purchase wheat flour, the germ has probably been removed by the miller. The germ contains oil that causes the flour to begin going rancid after three or four weeks at room temperature.

Wheat flour may be stored for several weeks at room temperature without losing substantial nutrition. This refutes the belief that freshly milled flour loses nutrient value quickly after milling. There is evidence that the baking process actually destroys more nutrients than those lost due to leaving wheat flour out at room temperature for a few days or even weeks. Technical data indicates that the chemical makeup of freshly-milled wheat flour, and its digestibility in the human body is of greater concern nutritionally than the amount of time that lapses between the time the wheat is milled and its use in baking.[2]

According to calculations done with current statistics, the actual nutrient loss of wheat flour in the baking process is very minimal as well.[3]

If desired, you may store wheat flour in the refrigerator or freezer. Remember to let the flour sit out and come to room temperature before using it to make bread.

Whole wheat flour may not be labeled to show its breadmaking quality. You can check the nutrient label on the package where the protein content is listed. If it is 16 % or above, the flour will probably make good wheat bread.

Whole wheat flour contains not only the endosperm of the wheat kernel, but a small amount of wheat germ, and a large amount of wheat bran. The germ and the bran are the components that cause so much difficulty in breadmaking with 100% whole wheat flour. Let's talk for a moment about wheat bran and wheat germ.

Wheat bran is very nutritious, and is rich in dietary fiber, as was mentioned earlier. However, after milling, wheat bran has rough, sharp edges that can damage the gluten framework of whole wheat dough as it is being kneaded, and also as it rises. With bran present in bread dough, the gluten also takes longer to develop than if it were absent (8-10 minutes of kneading wheat bread as opposed to 3-5 minutes of kneading white bread). For these reasons, I never add extra bran to whole wheat bread recipes.

The nutrition in wheat germ is also valuable in whole wheat bread. However, wheat germ contains, among other things, an agent called glutathione that breaks down gluten in whole wheat bread dough. The longer the germ is in contact with the gluten that has developed in bread dough, the more damage it can do to the dough. For this reason, I never add extra wheat germ to my wheat bread. As you read, you will learn other steps you can take to minimize the damage from the glutathione. We will discuss them further as the breadmaking process unfolds.

Substituting White and Other Flours

If you choose to substitute white flour for any of the wheat flour in your bread, there are some tips to remember. White flour purchased for use in breadmaking, should be labeled "Better for Bread," as opposed to "All-Purpose." All-purpose flour does not contain the strong gluten-making proteins that are contained in breadmaking flour. All purpose flour is used for making quick breads, cookies, cakes, and pie crusts, You don't want or need strong gluten strands in these types of baked goods.

Bleached white flour is derived from the endosperm layer of the wheat kernel. When commercial mills process wheat into white flour, the bran and the germ are removed (along with all of their nutrients). The remaining endosperm layer is bleached white (or left its natural off-white color for unbleached flour). Of the 16 nutrients that are removed from wheat flour when it is processed, only three major nutrients are reintroduced into the white flour (thiamin, riboflavin, and niacin). The addition of these nutrients has helped eradicate vitamin deficiency diseases such as pellegra. With the exception of these three nutrients, wheat flour contains more nutrients and fiber than processed white flour.[4]

Unbleached flour is not any more nutritious than bleached flour, although some people prefer using it because it hasn't undergone the bleaching process. Both bleached and unbleached flour are classified as white flour, although bleached flour is a little whiter in color.

There are two big reasons why white flour is used both privately and commercially for breadmaking, even though it is nutritionally inferior to wheat flour. During the mid 1600's, white bread

became the bread of royalty because of its light, delicate color and flavor. Consequently, common people began to wish for this luxury food, thereby creating a demand for white bread. White bread has been with us ever since that time. The second reason that white flour is used in breadmaking is because it is easier to get good results than with whole wheat flour. If you have ever made white bread, you know how easy it is to knead white bread dough, and how little time it takes to develop the gluten (three to five minutes by hand). With the bran and germ removed, there is nothing to impede the development of the proteins into long strands of gluten.

Up to one-third of the whole wheat flour in any bread recipe may be interchanged with either bleached or unbleached white flour.

If you want to substitute cracked wheat for some of your wheat flour, substitute for no more than one-eighth of your wheat flour. Be sure to cook the cracked wheat or soak it overnight to soften it.

Barley, rice, millet, oat, bean, and corn flour may be substituted for one-third of the wheat flour in any bread recipe. Each of these flours manifests unique characteristics. Consequently, the texture of your bread will be different from that of 100% whole wheat bread.

Rice and bean flours tend to be heavy, so use one-fourth or less of each of these ingredients.

Freshly ground rye flour may be used in place of one-sixth of the whole wheat flour.

YEAST

Yeast is a living plant that needs warmth and moisture to grow. Warm bread dough provides a perfect place for yeast growth, but yeast still needs food in a form that it can use. Yeast thrives best on sugar, so when yeast comes in contact with the flour in bread dough, enzymes in yeast convert the starch in flour into a sugar. Flour does not provide all the food yeast needs, so other yeast food is usually added to bread dough (sugar, honey, molasses). Yeast then ferments these sugars into alcohol and carbon dioxide gas. The gas is trapped in the gluten network, causing bread dough to rise. The process continues until the oxygen in the dough is used up. This fermentation process is desirable in the dough, for it gives bread a good flavor. However, if dough is left to rise too long, the yeast quits working as well, and the alcohol in the dough increases. This rising level of alcohol can kill the yeast. It also damages the gluten. The resulting loaf of bread will be compact, heavy, and will have a strong smell of alcohol. For this reason, watch your dough closely. If necessary, measure it as it rises to ensure that it never rises more than double its original size.

There are three different types of yeast available for purchase. The most powerful yeast with the greatest rising ability is compressed yeast. It is a little harder to find than the other types of yeast, but it is well worth the effort. It is more perishable than dry yeast, because the yeast cells are live and active, and must be used within six weeks. Because the yeast cells are alive and active, it may be added directly to bread dough. Make sure that the yeast is fresh. Then be sure to follow any other specific directions on each package of compressed yeast.

The next most powerful yeast to use is instant, rapid-rise yeast (SAF, Fermipan, Fleischmann's Rapid Rise Yeast). This yeast contains yeast cells that are alive but not active. The outer shell on each dry yeast granule is soft enough that it does not need to be pre-softened in warm water before being added to other bread ingredients. It will absorb liquid as it is mixed directly into the dough. It may be added to bread dough after the first one or two cups of flour are added.

The least powerful yeast for whole wheat breadmaking is regular active dry yeast (Fleischmann's, Red Star). The yeast cells are alive, but are not active. The outer shell on each yeast granule is very hard, and needs to be softened in warm water (85-110 degrees F.) for five to ten minutes before being added to other bread ingredients. Because it is less powerful than instant or compressed yeast, it takes 20-25% more of this yeast than the other two types to get the same results. You may want to add a half teaspoon sugar or molasses to the dissolving water; it gives yeast a little food to begin growing. If your yeast does not grow after five minutes, it may be old. In that case, you will need fresh yeast.

You will recall that wheat germ contains an agent called glutathione which breaks down the gluten in whole wheat bread dough. Interestingly, this agent is also present in yeast. Glutathione in the yeast will not affect the quality of your bread as long as it stays in the yeast cell. Only under adverse conditions will the glutathione leak out. Compressed yeast retains the strength of its yeast cells very effectively, and generally has little to no problems. If you are using active dry yeast, how ever, you need to be very careful that your dissolving water is no cooler than 100 degrees F. Glutathione will leak out of the yeast cells very rapidly in cool water, causing your dough strength to be weakened. Rapid-rise yeast, or instant yeast does not need to be dissolved in water. However, to avoid any unwanted glutathione release, make sure the dough, or flour temperature is 75 degrees or higher when adding instant yeast.[5] For this reason, I prefer using compressed or instant yeast. Not only are they more powerful, but they have less of a problem with glutathione release. Most of the recipes in this book will call for instant yeast.

If your freshly milled flour is very warm (over 120 degrees), make sure the liquid in your bread recipe is a little cooler than 90 degrees. Otherwise, the heat from the liquid, the heat from the flour, and the heat generated from kneading may overheat the dough and kill the yeast.

Purchasing and Storing Yeast

Purchase only fresh yeast, whether it is compressed, instant, or active dry yeast. Old yeast just does not perform well.

If you purchase compressed yeast, store it in the refrigerator, but do not allow it to freeze. Freezing temperatures will kill the live yeast cells.

Instant, fast-rise yeast, as well as active dry yeast, is sold in large quantity packages. The best place to store either type is unopened in a freezer  at 0-10 degrees F. A lower temperature could kill the yeast; a higher temperature will shorten its shelf life.

Once a large package of yeast is opened, it may be stored in small baby food jars (with tight lids) in the refrigerator. This allows only one small container to be used at a time. Constant exposure to air and moisture can cause yeast to lose its potency.

Active dry yeast is also sold in small envelopes (approximately 1 Tb. each), or in large quantity packages. The envelopes store best in a refrigerator.

Sourdough and Yeast Free Breads

If you have no yeast on hand, and want or need to make bread, wild yeast (or sourdough starter) may be used. Wild yeast grows from spores in the air. Some yeast spores respond very well in bread while others do not. For this reason, whole wheat breadmaking with wild yeast is always an adventure. If you desire to try it, refer to a good sourdough cookbook for instructions.

I've been asked about making yeast free bread.

Some home bakers try to make yeast bread without yeast, then allow the bread to sit for one or two days to rise naturally. Yeast spores from the air land on the bread dough, causing fermentation to occur, and natural yeast is created. Wheat bread dough also creates its own yeast. If you want bread that is really yeast free, it is probably best to find a good yeast-free cookbook for recipes that use baking powder or soda for leavening.

LIQUID

Water, milk, potato water, or buttermilk will fill the requirement for liquid in whole wheat bread.

Water allows the flavor of the wheat to be more pronounced, and is the least expensive of all the liquid ingredients.

Milk (including reconstituted powdered milk) causes the bread to toast more evenly and quickly. Milk can also cause the bread to rise higher and have a finer texture than water. Breads stay fresh longer when made with milk. However, any milk except evaporated milk needs to be scalded and cooled before use. Scalding the milk kills the enzymes that adversely soften bread dough.

Potato water gives greater volume, as milk does, but gives bread a coarse texture.

Buttermilk causes the dough to be more tender, and adds a distinctive flavor to wheat bread.

If you choose to use buttermilk in your bread, use buttermilk for half the liquid requirement and water or scalded milk for the rest. Too much buttermilk can make bread dough so tender that it falls apart. Also, make sure that you scald the buttermilk before using it. The culture can interfere with the yeast.

Yogurt can be substituted for one-fourth of the water or milk in a bread recipe. It needs to be scalded and cooled before using. It gives a strong yogurt flavor to wheat bread.

Oil and Fat

Oil or fat is used in bread to increase elasticity. It also produces a more tender crumb. Volume increases, bread browns more evenly, and stays fresh longer.

Because oil tenderizes dough, never use too much oil or fat in your bread. It will shorten the gluten strands in the bread, making it crumbly, with less volume. It will be more like cake (this may sound good, but have you ever tried to make a sandwich out of cake slices?).

One tablespoon of vegetable oil for each four cups of flour is sufficient.

Nutritionally speaking, none of us can afford to eat too much fat or oil. Excessive fat in the diet is being linked to higher incidents of heart disease and various cancers, as well as obesity. Health experts tell us that ideally, only 10-20% of our daily caloric intake should be in the form of fats or oils. By using one tablespoon of fat or oil for each four cups of flour, our bread will contain 12% fat (five percent of that fat occurs naturally in the wheat germ, leaving only seven percent from the added oil). If bread needs a little fat or oil as one of the ingredients, use only what is necessary, and not an excess.

There are two factors to consider when deciding which oil or fat to use in your bread. One factor is nutrition. Which oil or fat will be the most healthy? The other factor is success in breadmaking. Which oil or fat will produce the best result in the bread?

Nutritionally speaking, the most healthy oil to use is lecithin, derived from soybeans. Not only is it rich in nutrients, but it is known to help emulsify cholesterol in the body, which lowers the cholesterol level.

Vegetable oils (such as corn, sunflower, or

sesame oil) are also healthy to use in breadmaking. Vegetable oil in small amounts may actually be beneficial to the heart and arteries.

Butter may be used to fill the fat requirement. Some health experts believe, however, that because butter is high in cholesterol, and is a saturated fat, that it should be used very sparingly, if at all. Others claim that because it is a natural product, without a lot of chemicals introduced into it, the body is able to assimilate it with no ill effect. You will have to choose whether or not to use butter in your breadmaking. Some of the recipes in the automatic breadmaker section call for butter. If desired, you may substitute lecithin or vegetable oil (use one-third more oil than butter; use only half the amount of lecithin).

The least nutritious of the fats is lard and shortening. Lard is basically animal fat. Shortening is usually made from vegetable oil which has had hydrogen introduced into it to make it solid. The hydrogenation process creates a prod-

uct which, like lard, is linked to serious heart disease and various cancers. If you choose to use either of these two types of fat, do so sparingly.

The other factor to consider when choosing your oil or fat is product success. I prefer using lecithin in my bread not only for its nutritional benefits, but for the binding quality it has on bread dough. The solid portion of lecithin, not the oil, acts as the binder in wheat bread. For this reason, powdered lecithin is better (and more convenient) than liquid lecithin, although it is harder to find. Consequently, the recipes in this book call for liquid lecithin. A teaspoon and a half of liquid lecithin per loaf is sufficient as a binder. However, a different type of vegetable oil or fat is needed to produce a tender crumb. Any recipes in this book calling for lecithin also call for additional vegetable oil. For greater ease when using liquid lecithin, measure it into the additional vegetable oil, then add both to the recipe together.

If you are able to find powdered lecithin, follow the label directions for proper amounts, or substitute equally for liquid lecithin.

There are times when I want my bread to be exceptionally tender (for gift giving, or for special occasions). When this is the case, I choose to use butter or shortening that is at room temperature. I use one-third less butter than oil, because oil absorbs into flour at a higher rate than butter. Butter, if mixed into dough while soft, but still in a solid state, coats the gluten without totally absorbing into the flour. It helps the dough to rise more easily, and creates a more tender loaf during the baking process.

Whether you use oil or fat, make sure that it is fresh. Rancid oil or fat should never be used in breadmaking.

Bread can be made without any oil or fat, as in the case of sourdough bread. The dough will be a little less elastic, and the finished loaves will have a dry, coarse texture.

There is one other way that fats are used in breadmaking. Shortening has been used for years to grease pans, and oil has been used to lubricate the surface of bread dough as it rises. I prefer using a spray-on cooking oil. There are several brands available in grocery stores, PAM™ being the most common. It is easier to use than shortening, contains fewer fat grams than shortening, and is made with lecithin, a very nutritious oil. For this reason, my bread pans and bread bowls are sprayed rather than greased or oiled.

SALT

Salt brings out the flavor of the other ingredients in the bread. It also controls the fermentation process. If you have ever made bread and left out the salt, you may have encountered bread that rose too high, then collapsed on itself. Not only was the bread tasteless, but flat as well. If salt needs to be deleted for health reasons, be sure to watch the dough carefully that it doesn't rise too high at any stage.

Salt should never be added to the liquid in which the yeast is dissolving, because it may inhibit or kill the yeast.

SUGAR

Sugar feeds the yeast and adds flavor to the bread. Too little sugar can prevent oven browning, while too much sugar causes excess oven browning. This is helpful to know whenever you choose to alter any recipe. White sugar, brown sugar, honey, or molasses may be used, although molasses is an especially good food for yeast.

When using honey in your recipe, use a little sugar with the honey (for every one quarter cup of honey, add one teaspoon sugar). It will provide

food for the yeast and leave the sweetness of the honey to flavor the bread.

WHEN OPTIONAL INGREDIENTS ARE NEEDED

The only additional ingredient that may be necessary to the success of your bread is gluten flour. It is listed as an optional ingredient, however, because it is not always needed. As you read through the section describing gluten flour, and its use in whole wheat bread, you will know just when it is needed.

The other ingredients listed here are truly optional. If you correctly apply the basic principles of whole wheat breadmaking, your bread should turn out very well. The use of optional ingredients will just enhance something that is already good.

If you experience poor results without the use of optional ingredients, I suspect that one of the basics is lacking.

Re-check the protein content of your wheat, then each step of the process. When you have achieved satisfaction, begin to experiment with the ingredients described below.

GLUTEN FLOUR

Gluten flour (also called vital wheat gluten) is extracted from high protein wheat. The wheat is milled and the bran and germ are removed. The starch is then washed away, leaving the gluten. It is dried and milled into flour. When added to bread dough, it acts as a binder to make dough more elastic and keep bread from crumbling.

If your wheat flour is lower than 16% protein, you will need to add gluten flour to your bread. Otherwise, your bread will not hold together well, and it will not rise very high. If your wheat flour is 16-20% protein, you have a little more freedom to decide whether or not to use gluten flour. I prefer using gluten flour in all of my whole wheat breads, even if the protein in my flour is above 16%. This is just my personal preference. Nevertheless, anything below 16% protein must have more protein added in the form of gluten flour, as a minimum standard.

If your wheat is milled too coarsely, the gluten that naturally occurs in the wheat flour will not develop properly during kneading. You can soften the flour by soaking it in water overnight, but the gluten will not develop any better. In this case, gluten flour will help bind the bread together to keep it from crumbling.

The process of kneading develops gluten. If you are unable to knead your bread long enough to develop the gluten, your bread will have large cells, and will crumble very easily after baking. If this is the case, gluten flour will help ensure that your bread will not fall apart when it is sliced.

After wheat is milled into flour, the bran may have sharp, jagged edges that can damage the gluten in your bread. Adding extra gluten flour may help compensate for this damage to the dough.

Sometimes, automatic breadmakers don't knead wheat bread dough long enough totally to develop the gluten. In this case, extra gluten flour will help bind the bread together.

Too much gluten flour in a recipe can make the bread tough and rubbery, so be careful not to use too much. Most recipes in this book will call for gluten flour, simply because it is easier to omit gluten flour from your recipe if you don't need it than to guess how much to use if you do need it.

Two or three tablespoons of gluten flour may

be added for each loaf of wheat bread if you choose to use it. Unless a different amount is indicated in a recipe, this amount will generally be sufficient.

Gluten flour may be found in most health food stores, bakeries, wheat outlets, or mill shops.

ASCORBIC ACID

Ascorbic acid, or Vitamin C, helps sustain the leavening of bread loaves during baking.

Ascorbic acid also helps counteract the negative effects of wheat germ. As was mentioned earlier, wheat germ (and active dry yeast, to a small degree) contains a reducing agent called glutathione. This agent breaks down gluten in wheat bread (after you've worked so hard to develop it). Ascorbic acid will not only help prevent the gluten from breaking down, but will help to repair gluten bonds that have already been broken. The benefits of ascorbic acid are more pronounced when flour is low in protein.

When you allow bread dough to rise more than one time, the wheat germ has more opportunity to work against the gluten in the dough. If you are going to allow your bread dough to rise more than one time (and certainly if you have used active dry yeast), be sure to add ascorbic acid to your bread recipe.

For a large bread recipe that calls for 24 cups of flour, add 50-200 mg. of ascorbic acid to the liquid in the recipe (use the larger amount if you have low protein flour). If you make a small batch of bread (two loaves), add 15-65 mg. of ascorbic acid.

The easiest way to use ascorbic acid is to buy it in 25-50 mg. tablets, then dissolve it in the water for your recipe (do not dissolve it in milk; it will curdle the milk). You may also mill it right along with your flour.

DOUGH ENHANCER

Dough enhancer may contain any combination of whey, ascorbic acid or vitamin C, salt, cornstarch, lecithin, tofu, and flavorings (as well as other ingredients). Sometimes, the ingredients in dough enhancer provide food for the yeast (depending on the exact ingredients). Some components in dough enhancer (especially ascorbic acid) repair and strengthen the gluten in bread dough, which improves the quality of the bread.

When dough enhancer is used, ascorbic acid is not usually necessary, and vice versa.

WHEY

Whey is a dairy by-product rich in protein and minerals, and high in milk sugar. It sweetens the dough slightly and aids browning in the oven. Add whey to your wheat bread if you want a lighter, more delicate color of bread. Add one-fourth to one-third cup whey per loaf.

EGGS

Eggs enhance whole wheat bread in several ways. As mentioned earlier, lecithin may be used in wheat bread for the binding quality it has on bread dough. In the absence of lecithin, one egg per loaf of bread will act on bread in the same way (lecithin occurs naturally in egg yolks).

Eggs also add a rich golden color to bread while improving the texture. Eggs cause bread also to rise higher, and stay fresh longer. Decrease liquid in the recipe by one-fourth cup for each egg.

POTATOES

It may seem a little unusual that I would include potatoes as an optional ingredient in whole wheat bread. Actually, potatoes are a good source of yeast food, as well as Vitamin C. When cooked, mashed, then added to bread dough, potatoes act as a dough enhancer. Does the name "Spudnuts™" ring a bell? The original Spudnut doughnuts contained just that—good old spuds. Do you remember how light and fluffy those doughnuts were? When added to wheat bread, mashed potatoes really do make a lighter, better-textured bread. One-fourth cup of mashed potatoes per loaf may be added. If the mashed potatoes are the same consistency as table-ready mashed potatoes, the liquid in the recipe should stay constant. If the potatoes are a little runny, decrease water by two tablespoons for each one-fourth

cup of mashed potatoes.

You may be tempted to use potato flakes or granules in place of mashed potatoes. Neither of these will have the same beneficial effect as freshly cooked potatoes.

DIASTATIC, NON-DIASTATIC MALTS (BARLEY, TRITICALE, ETC.)

I mention these malts, not to encourage their use, but to dispel myths about their use.

Barley or other malts may be used as sweetening agents in bread. There are other uses for malts in bread also. However, they may have enzymes present that damage starches or proteins in bread. Professional bakers use various malts, but they also have the proper testing equipment to ensure the results they want. There are enough variables to address when using malts that I discourage their use in homemade wheat bread until a tried and tested product is available for home use.

Using optional ingredients can improve the quality and texture of homemade bread, but the cost per loaf increases. Experiment with these optional ingredients and judge for yourself if the benefit is worth the additional cost.

MIXING AND KNEADING DOUGH

HAND MIXING AND KNEADING

Breadmaking is truly an art for those who choose to make bread the old fashioned way—by hand. There is a wonderfully therapeutic effect when you work your hands through bread dough, making sure by feeling, working, and molding the dough, just when the gluten is perfectly developed. Life seems to be a little richer when we take the time to feel, enjoy, and to immerse ourselves in the process rather than constantly hurrying to just get it done.

You may make bread by hand only because you have no breadmixer. Fortunately, the process is enjoyable and relaxing. You also have the advantage of being able to tell if your dough is kneaded enough by really working with it, and not just looking at it. You will also have peace of mind and pride in your ability to make good bread by hand.

When making bread without an electric or manual bread mixer, a few simple tips can ensure success.

If the recipe calls for six to eight cups of flour, add only four or five cups flour at first. Then add only enough flour while kneading to keep the dough from sticking to the kneading surface and to your hands. The amount of flour used will vary according to humidity in the air, moisture content in the flour, and the type flour used. If the air is humid, you may need more flour. If you live in a dry climate and your flour is very dry, you may need less flour. If your flour is high in protein, you will generally use less than if the flour is low in protein.

If too much flour is added while kneading, the dough will be very hard to handle. The resulting bread will be dry and crumbly. There have been times when I could tell that my dough was too dry, and I tried to add more water after I had been kneading for a few minutes. It's very hard to get the water incorporated again by hand, so be very careful as you begin adding flour; do not add too much too soon.

If your dough is consistently too dry or too sticky, a good kitchen scale can help. Weighing ingredients on a scale is always more accurate than using measuring cups and spoons. You can consistently duplicate your successes, because you'll be able to weigh your ingredients so that they are exact every time you make bread.

Kneading becomes easier if you develop a rhythm as you knead. As the dough is worked, it will become smooth on the outside surface. Avoid tearing or breaking through this surface. It will damage the gluten strands that are developing.

Firmly pushing the dough brings the best results. Pounding the dough with a mallet is another good way to develop the gluten.

Dough has been kneaded enough when it is smooth, satiny, and elastic to the touch. It will generally take 10-15 minutes of good, hard kneading to develop the gluten in the flour properly. Many batches of bread (including my own first few batches) result in very crumbly bread because the dough has not been kneaded enough. The higher the protein content of your flour, the longer it takes to develop gluten during the kneading process. Fourteen percent protein flour may only take 10 minutes of kneading, while 16% protein flour may take 15 minutes.

Remember to add gluten flour to your bread recipe if you find that you aren't able to knead the bread dough long enough to develop the gluten sufficiently.

If the dough seems stiff and hard to handle during kneading, instead of pliable and elastic, pick it up and throw it onto the kneading surface a few times. It will relax the dough, and you'll spend less time kneading.

After kneading bread dough, there is a quick and easy test that will tell you if the gluten has been adequately developed. Take a half cup of dough and stretch it gently until you can see light through it. If it tears easily while stretching, the gluten is underdeveloped. If the dough holds together without tearing, the gluten is properly developed.

Machine Mixing and Kneading

When using a breadmixer to mix and knead your dough, it takes a few batches of bread to become familiar with your machine. For instance, some breadmixers knead the dough so rapidly that if you are not careful, your dough will be completely kneaded before you've had time to add all the flour needed in the recipe. So go slowly with your mixer at first as you become familiar with how it works.

Choose a recipe, then follow the recipe instructions for putting the ingredients together. When all the ingredients have been added in your mixer, along with about half of the flour, turn the machine on low speed, blending the ingredients together. If you are making only two or three loaves of bread, you'll need to add only about one-half cup of flour at a time as the dough mixes. If you are making five or six loaves, you may add one cup of flour at a time as the dough mixes. Keep adding flour, a little at a time, until the dough begins to pull away from the sides of the mixing bowl. Stop adding flour for a moment, until all the existing flour is well incorporated into the dough. Stop the machine if necessary and feel the dough. If the dough holds its shape when a small handful is carefully pulled our of the bowl, it is ready to knead without adding more flour. If the dough is still very sticky, and seems to slide down the center post of the mixing bowl, then it needs more flour. When the dough pulls almost completely away from the bowl, it means that the gluten is developing, and is just about the right texture. If your machine is a heavy-duty mixer, allow it to knead until the dough is smooth and elastic.

If your machine begins to labor, it may be normal for your machine, or it may be that too much flour has been added to your dough, making it stiff and dry. This is not only hard on the breadmixer, but your finished bread will be compact, heavy, dry, and crumbly.

If your machine is not heavy or big enough to knead the dough completely, and the dough is not too stiff, you may remove the dough from the mixer. Continue kneading it by hand on a smooth surface which has been lightly coated with flour, until it is smooth, shiny, and the gluten is fully developed.

If you allow your breadmixer to knead too long, the dough will begin to tear instead of stretch as it kneads. At this point, the gluten has been damaged, and cannot be repaired. The dough will tear easily as it is formed into loaves, and it will not rise as high as it should.

Once the dough is kneaded, let it rest for five or ten minutes before molding it into loaves. If it needs to rise once before the loaves are formed, it may be placed in a sprayed bowl immediately.

Bread On The Rise

You may now see the dilemma that whole wheat breadmakers face. The full, rich flavor of wheat bread is achieved by allowing several fermentation (rising) periods. Also, gluten is developed further by more than one rising period. Yet, when gluten (that has just been developed through kneading) is constantly exposed to the glutathione in the wheat germ and regular yeast, (as well as the sharp edges of the bran) during these rising periods, it breaks down, and the bread may become compact and heavy. You end up with a brick that is very flavorful!

I believe that whole wheat bread is the very best, considering all the variables, when it has only one, or at most, two rising periods. This is very different from what we've heard for years about whole wheat breadmaking; that bread gets better with each rising period. Although the flavor may get better, the loft and lightness of the loaf gradually decreases with each rising period. When machine kneading, one rising period is enough. When hand kneading, a second rising allows further gluten development.

If you make bread that needs only one rising period in the pans, remember to keep the dough warm (68-82 degrees F.) while rising (although it will probably still be sufficiently warm from the kneading). However, if temperatures are too warm (above 100 degrees F.) while rising in the pans, the dough may rise too rapidly, causing the finished loaves to be dense at the bottom and crumbly at the top.

If you make bread that needs to rise more than once, place the kneaded dough in a large bowl that has been lightly sprayed. Lightly spray the top of the dough also, then cover it with a warm, damp cloth. Make sure that it is placed in a draft-free location.

After the dough has risen until it has doubled in size (anywhere from 45 minutes to 1-1/2 hours), you can test the dough to see if it is ready to be punched down. Push your index finger about two inches into the dough (very quickly). If the hole you've made stays in the dough without filling in, the dough is ready to punch down. If the hole closes in a little, the dough is not ready. It needs a little more time to ferment. Use this test only on the first rising.

If the dough completely collapses when you test it with your finger, it has risen too long. In fact, if dough is allowed to rise too high at any stage of the breadmaking process, the bread will collapse on itself, and will not rise again. The damage is irreparable. Bread will be crumbly, will smell of alcohol, and will be heavy (thus the term "hard as a brick"). You will be better off using the dough to make scones rather than loaves of bread.

Once dough has risen enough, it needs to be punched down. Gently push your fist down into the center of the dough. Then pull the edges of the dough in toward the center. Punch down the dough that is left around the edges, then turn the dough over. Let it rest for a few minutes. It may then be shaped and placed in sprayed bread pans.

By the time the dough begins to rise again in the pans, the dough will be cooler than during the first rising period. If the dough is too cool, the dough may not rise well, and the loaves will stay compact. A towel may be folded and placed directly beneath the bread pans. This helps insulate the dough. Also, a warm, damp towel may be placed over the top of the rising dough (not only does the warmth help the dough to rise better, but the dampness improves the texture of the finished crust).

There is a way to test the dough in the pans to see if it is oven ready. Press your index finger into the dough at the edge of the loaf, next to the pan. Do not press in more than one-fourth inch. If the dent fills back in immediately, the bread is not ready to bake. If the dent very slowly returns to normal, or almost normal, the bread is ready to bake. If the dent does not fill in, the dough has risen too long, and the bread may collapse in the oven. Generally, you can also tell by looking at your loaves if they are oven ready. They will be about double in size, and the dough will have risen just above the top of the pan.

Saving Dough for Later Use

While making bread, you may find that you have to leave your breadmaking unexpectedly. Bread dough may be refrigerated any time after it has been kneaded and before it is baked. If left for only and hour or two, the bread will probably be fine. If left overnight, the yeast will use up most of its food, and the wheat germ will further break down the gluten. The bread will be more compact and heavy after baking, but heavy bread is better than no bread!

Make sure that the dough is punched down well, then place it in a large bowl that has been lightly sprayed with PAM™. Cover it tightly with plastic wrap and place it in the back of the refrigerator until you are able to finish making bread. You will have to punch the dough down several times if it stays in the refrigerator overnight. Do not save the dough more than one day. When it comes out of the refrigerator, it will take several hours to come up to room temperature. After the dough warms for several hours, mold it into loaves and place it into greased or sprayed pans to rise. It will take several more hours for dough to rise enough to bake.

SHAPING THE LOAVES

Bread dough needs to rest for about 10 minutes before being shaped into loaves. This gives the dough time to relax, and it is much easier to shape the loaves.

There are several ways to shape the dough. One way is to gently divide the bread dough with your hands (without tearing the dough) into the number of loaves you plan to make. If you have a kitchen scale, you can weigh your the dough for each loaf. Each ball of dough should weigh 1-1/2 pounds if you are using standard size pans.

If you do not have a kitchen scale, you may use a one-half cup size measuring cup with a long handle on it to gently divide out one-half cup size pieces of dough from the larger dough mass (lightly spray the measuring cup first). It will take six of these small balls of dough to form a standard loaf of wheat bread.

After measuring the amount of dough needed for each loaf, take the premeasured dough and roll it out on a slightly sprayed or oiled counter into a rectangle, 7-1/2 " by 10". Then roll the narrow end up, jelly-roll fashion, pinching the seam together. Place the dough into a sprayed pan and cover it with a damp towel. Never use vegetable oil to coat your bread pans (especially if they are aluminum). The bread may bake right on to the pan!

Another way to shape the dough is to place the dough for each loaf on a lightly sprayed counter. For each loaf of bread, pound the dough with your fist into a tight ball to eliminate air bubbles. Then place the ball of dough in the center of a sprayed pan, and cover it with a towel. Even though you are pounding the dough into a ball, take care that you do not tear the dough.

Some people have good luck just breaking out a chunk of dough, smoothing out the top, and placing it in a sprayed pan. I don't seem to have very good luck with this method. I always end up with oddly shaped bread. Sometimes when I am in a hurry, and this is my only option, it may be quite humorous to see what my finished loaves look like, both inside and out.

Varying Crust Textures

For a shiny, chewy crust, dissolve 1 tsp. cornstarch in 2/3 c. water and bring to a boil. Let it cool slightly, then brush on loaves before baking. Repeat after the first 10 minutes of baking.

For a golden crust, brush loaves with a beaten egg just before baking.

For a crust with seeds, brush the loaves with beaten egg white. Then sprinkle with sesame, poppy, or dill seeds. Egg white also gives a shiny finish.

Baking, Cooling, and Slicing Bread

Bread should be baked at a high temperature (400 degrees F) for 10-15 minutes. This sets the yeast cells and prevents the loaves from rising any higher. The oven temperature can then be decreased to 350 degrees to finish the baking process.

You may be tempted to bake your bread at 325 degrees for the entire baking period (for instance, if you have to leave the house during the baking period). If the yeast cells in the dough are not immediately set by the high oven temperature (400 degrees), the bread may rise too high in the oven and create an air pocket just below the top crust. Also, the loaf may be dense at the bottom, and so light and airy at the top that it crumbles easily. After the bread bakes at the higher temperature for 10-15 minutes, the oven must then be turned to a lower temperature to complete the baking. If kept at the higher temperature longer than 10-15 minutes, the bread will over bake, and will be dry and hard.

Because wheat bread is brown to begin with (or at least darker than white bread), it sometimes will get too brown in the oven. If you like the crust on your wheat bread a little lighter, cover the loaves with aluminum foil during the last 15-20 minutes of baking (shiny side up).

A well-formed loaf of bread can suddenly develop an uneven shape while baking, because of uneven oven heat. A crack can develop along one side, or the loaf will hang over one side of the pan. The crack will develop on the side which has the lowest oven temperature. Make sure that there is a space between the loaves in the oven so that the heat can circulate evenly between the loaves.

ALTITUDE AND CLIMATE ADJUSTMENTS

If you live above the 4,000 foot level, there is less atmospheric pressure to "push down" on bread dough. Standard bread recipes may need to be altered, using less yeast (about twenty-five percent less). Rising periods will be shorter, and the bread will need to be baked at a higher temperature. For example, at high altitudes, bread may need to bake at 425 degrees for 10 minutes, than at 350 degrees for 25 minutes. At lower altitudes, bread bakes best at 400 degrees for the first 10 minutes, then at 350 degrees for 25-30 minutes.

If you live in a dry climate, less flour may be needed. In a moist climate, more flour may be needed. Be willing to experiment a little.*

COOLING BREAD

When bread comes out of the oven, it needs to come out of the pans within five minutes. Otherwise the bread may become soggy under-

*The recipes in this book were formulated at 4500 ft. above sea level. If you live higher, or lower than 4500 ft, adjust accordingly.

neath. The loaves may be brushed with melted butter, margarine, or heavy cream while still hot. This leaves a soft, shiny crust. Cool on a rack, then put away in clean plastic bread sacks.

Hot bread may be dashed quickly under running water. Steam will be created, leaving a soft crust. Another way to create a soft crust is to cool the bread for only 5-10 minutes. Place in a plastic bread sack with the end open to allow excess steam to escape. When the bread is cool, remove it from the plastic sack, wipe excess moisture off the bread with a clean towel, then place in a clean, dry bread sack.

Whole wheat bread will stay fresh for one day at room temperature, two or three days in a refrigerator, or up to three months in a freezer, if well wrapped.

SLICING BREAD

Slicing your bread can be a mouth-watering experience, or it may be a miserable trial. The knife you use will be the deciding factor. The best knife to use when slicing bread is a long, sharp serrated knife. If you keep your bread knife for slicing bread, and nothing else, it will stay sharp for a long time.

If your bread is still hot when you slice it, your slices will need to be a little thicker than normal, because the cell walls of the bread are very fragile until the bread cools. Be gentle with the knife. Use a sawing action, going back and forth at least 7 or 8 times before reaching the bottom of the loaf. Try to slice without pushing down too hard on the loaf.

Once the bread has cooled, it is still important to use a sharp, serrated knife. The bread isn't as fragile, but you'll still have better luck slicing with a good knife

BREADMAKER INSTRUCTIONS (SINGLE LOAVES)

An automatic breadmaker is wonderfully convenient for breadmaking, but it is not totally automatic when making 100% whole wheat bread. Most breadmakers are programmed to make white bread. Whole wheat bread may need a longer kneading time, more liquid, or a longer rising time than white bread. We'll go over these variables that need to be addressed so that the necessary adjustments can be made.

PROTEIN CONTENT

If you decide to make whole wheat bread in your machine, your wheat flour must be high in protein (16-20% protein is ideal). This is probably the single most important factor to consider when making wheat bread in a breadmaker.

MEASUREMENT OF INGREDIENTS

In my large bread-mixer, I can make one loaf of bread or six loaves. My machine is large enough for a lot of variation. A breadmaker is very limited in size, and there isn't much room for fluctuations in measurements. This is why most breadmakers come equipped with measuring utensils. If even one-half cup too much flour is used, or one-half tsp. too much yeast, the bread may not turn out.

The best way to ensure correct measuring is to use a kitchen scale to weigh your ingredients. With a little practice, you'll know exactly how much flour and liquid to use (especially if you use the same type wheat for each loaf).

If you do not have a small kitchen scale, at least try to use the same measuring utensils each time you bake in your breadmaker (also use the same type of wheat each time).

If you happen to use freshly-milled wheat

flour, and you do not have a kitchen scale, tap each cupful of flour on the counter a few times in order for the flour to settle, then add another spoonful or two of flour to make the full cup measurement. Freshly milled flour has a lot of air in it, and if it isn't tapped down a little, it will give you less flour in your recipe than is actually needed. I've had more than one loaf of bread fall because it was short on flour, even though I thought I had measured accurately. Be sure that you don't tap the flour down too much; you may end up with too much flour. Two or three taps on the counter should be plenty.

When using even the most exact measurements, you may look into your breadmaker during the kneading process and see your dough just going around and around in a little ball on top of the kneading arm. The dough is too dry, and needs more liquid. Add a tablespoonful of water at a time while the dough is kneading until the dough is pliable enough to be kneading instead of just spinning around (it takes a few minutes for the water to incorporate—be patient). If it takes very long to get the dough to a good consistency, you may need to start the kneading process again. Gluten just doesn't develop well in a spin!

At times I have been very exact in my measurements, yet after five minutes of kneading, the dough in the breadmaker is still too sticky. Add one-fourth cup of flour at a time until the dough is a better texture (it takes time and experience to figure out what a good-textured dough looks like in your machine; be persistent).

OVERNIGHT TIMING

When using your timer for overnight baking, measure the liquid, salt, sweetener, and oil into the breadmaker. Then add flour, optional ingredients, and yeast. The bran in the flour will absorb more moisture than usual because of the extended contact with the water. This will cause your bread to be dry and crumbly. Add 1/4 to 1/2 cup more liquid per loaf to your recipe.

TIME TO DEVELOP GLUTEN

When making white bread in a breadmaker, it generally takes 30-35 minutes of kneading to develop the gluten. Because of the bran present in wheat flour, it may take an additional 10-20 minutes of kneading to develop the gluten. The ideal is to have a breadmaker that can be programmed to knead for the additional time needed.

If your breadmaker is not programmable, you may stop your machine after the first (and second, if there is one) kneading process, and start over so that the wheat bread gets the extra kneading time it requires.

If after trying wheat bread a few times in your breadmaker, your gluten just isn't developing enough, you have the option of adding gluten flour to your dough. Too much gluten flour can make your bread rubbery and tough, so experiment a little and find what is right for your particular type flour (two or three tablespoons of gluten flour for each four cups of whole wheat flour should be sufficient).

RISE TIME

Whole wheat bread sometimes needs more time to rise than white bread. For this reason, be sure to use a strong, quick-rising yeast. Compressed or instant yeast will work much better in breadmaker bread than regular, active dry yeast.

Also, be sure to use wheat flour that is very high in protein. It makes dough that rises quicker and higher than low protein flour.

Some breadmaker manufacturers recommend increasing the amount of yeast when making whole wheat bread (as compared with white bread). You will need to experiment a little. If I use high protein wheat flour (16-18%), and use extra yeast as well, my dough sometimes rises way too high. Find out what your wheat flour will do for you before you add extra yeast.

It is also helpful if your breadmaker allows extra rising time for whole wheat bread. If it doesn't have this particular feature, there are some tips that will help. First of all, make sure that your yeast is fresh, and has been measured correctly. Then make sure that your liquid is barely warm to the touch, and your other ingredients are at room temperature, or a little warmer. This causes your dough to begin rising right away after it kneads, rather than taking up some of the rise time to get up to room temperature. Some breadmakers are equipped with a preheating cycle that warms all the ingredients to the ideal temperature before the kneading cycle begins. This can help give ALL the rise time to the actual rising.

BAKING TIME

In baking white bread, it is relatively easy to regulate the crust color. Because wheat bread is brown even before it is baked, it is common to have bread that is too brown by the time it is baked. Most breadmakers allow a choice of light, medium, or dark crust during the baking process. You may want to try baking wheat bread on the light setting.

CHAPTER TWO

BASIC WHEAT BREAD TECHNIQUES

Now you are ready to learn the basic method of making whole wheat bread. Be sure to read the recipe through twice before starting your bread.

If your wheat or flour is lower than 14% protein, add 1 extra tablespoon gluten flour per loaf of bread in addition to amount called for in recipe.

HAND-KNEADED BREAD TECHNIQUES (2 LOAVES)

Measure out liquid into large mixing bowl as you mill 5-6 cups wheat.

3 c. warm water (110 degrees—barely warm to the touch) *or*
3 1/4 c. scalded and cooled milk.

If using instant yeast, add 1 1/2 Tb. yeast after the second cup of flour. If using regular yeast, add 2 Tb. or two packages to water and allow to dissolve (5-10 minutes).

Add to warm water or milk:
2 Tb. sugar
2 Tb. oil or 4 t. fat
1 1/2 Tb. salt
2 cups whole wheat flour
Add yeast, then add 2 more cups flour.

Any or all of the following optional ingredients may be added to the recipe, with excellent results:

1 egg (decrease liquid by 1/4 cup) or 1 T. lecithin in place of 1 T. oil
3 Tb. gluten flour
50 mg. ascorbic acid or
1 T. dough enhancer

1/2 c. whey
2 Tb. molasses or honey
1/2 c. mashed potatoes

1. Stir mixture until smooth. Add 3-4 more cups flour.

2. Knead until smooth, shiny, and satiny, being careful to add only enough flour while kneading to keep dough from sticking to board and hands (10-15 minutes, or approximately 300 kneadings).

Dough that is a little stiff is ideal. Dough that is too soft will fall over the sides of your loaf pans as is rises and bakes.

3. For the quick method, shape dough into 2 loaves, place in sprayed pans, and allow to rise until double. Bake as directed below.

(3). For a slower method, place dough into sprayed bowl, then lightly spray the top of the dough. Cover, allowing dough to rise until double. Punch down, allow to rest 10 minutes, then shape into loaves and place into sprayed pans. Allow to rise until double (cover while rising with warm, damp towel).

4. Bake in preheated oven at 400 degrees for 10 minutes, then lower temperature to 350 degrees for 25-35 minutes.

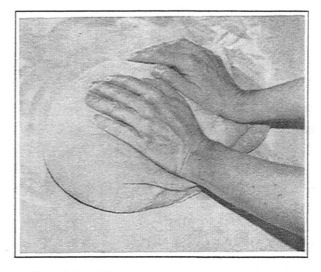

1. Knead by folding dough and pushing away with the heel of your hand, developing a quick rocking motion. Turn dough a quarter turn, repeating until gluten is developed.

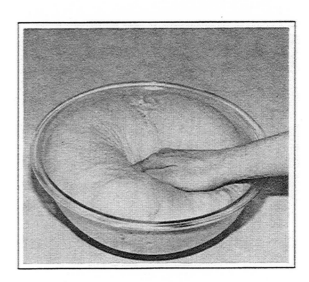

2. *Place dough in sprayed bowl, then lightly spray top of dough. Cover and let rise until double (45 minutes to 1 1/2 hours).*

3. *Punch down in center, pull edges in. Let rest 10 minutes.*

4. Break out 1/2 cup size pieces of dough (standard size pans hold 3 cups dough; baby pans hold 1 cup).

5. With fist, pound dough into a tight ball to eliminate air bubbles, then place in center of sprayed pan.

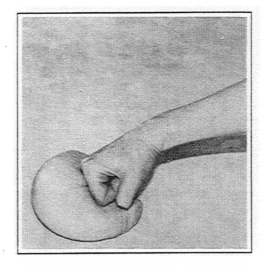

6. Measured dough can be rolled to the same width as the bread pan.

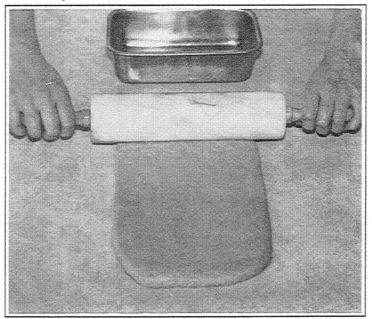

7. Roll dough up, jelly-roll fashion, pinching seam together.

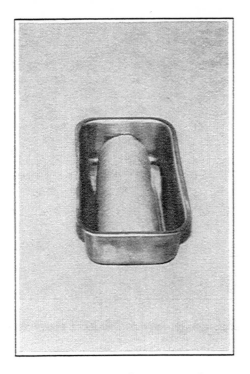

9. Bread is ready to bake if a slight dent remains when touched.

8. Place dough in center of pan, seam down. Cover and allow to rise until double.

BREADMAKER BREAD TECHNIQUES
(1 LOAF)

	Large	Medium	Small
Instant Yeast	2 t.	1 1/2 t.	1 t.
Wheat Flour	3 1/2 c.	2 1/2 c.	1 3/4 c.
Gluten Flour	2 T.	1 1/2 T.	1 T.
Sugar or honey	2 T.	1 1/2 T	1 T.
Salt	1 1/2 t.	1 t.	3/4 t.
Oil	1 1/2 T.	1 T.	2 2/3 t.
Lecithin	1 1/2 t.	1 t.	3/4 t.
Lukewarm Water	1 1/2 c.	1 1/8 c.	3/4 c.

OPTIONAL INGREDIENTS

	Large	Medium	Small
Dough Enhancer	1 1/2 t.	1 t.	3/4 t.
or Ascorbic Acid	25 mg.	20 mg.	15 mg.
Whey	1/4 c.	3 T.	2 T.
Molasses	2 T.	1 1/2 T.	1 T.
(instead of sugar)			

Measure the water first into the breadmaker. Measure the flour and other ingredients next, with the yeast being last. If you desire to use any optional ingredients, please be sure to follow the directions included with your particular breadmaker as well.

Select the proper setting, as outlined in your breadmaker instructions. Press the start button, and proceed until completed.

DOUGH SETTING

Any recipe desired can be mixed on the dough setting. When the dough cycle is complete, the dough can be removed from the machine, and used for rolls, breadsticks, hamburger, or hot dog buns.

The breadmaker basic recipe section would not be complete, however, without a recipe for cinnamon rolls. Following is a mouth-watering version especially for whole wheat enthusiasts.

BREADMAKER CINNAMON ROLLS

	Large	Medium	Small
Dough:			
Warm Milk	2/3 c.	1/2 c.	1/3 c.
Warm Water	1/2 c.	3/8 c.	1/4 c
Eggs	2	1	1
Sugar	3 T.	2 1/4 T.	1 1/2 T.
Melted Butter	1/4 c.	3 T.	2 T.
Wheat Flour	3 3/8 c.	2 1/2 c.	1 3/4 c.
Gluten Flour	2 T.	1 1/2 T.	1 T.
Instant Yeast	2 t.	1 1/2 t.	1 t.
Filling:			
Melted Butter	1/2 c.	6 T.	1/4 c.
Sugar	1/2 c.	6 T.	1/4 c.
Cinnamon	1 T.	3/4 T.	1/2 T.
Brown Sugar	1/2 c.	6 T.	1/4 c.
Chopped Nuts	1 c.	3/4 c.	1/2 c.
Raisins	1/2 c.	1/3 c.	1/4 c.

Icing:			
Powdered Sugar	2 c.	1 1/2 c.	1 c.
Corn Syrup	2 T.		
Orange or Lemon Juice	1/4 c.	3 T.	2 T.

Soak raisins in hot water until plump. Drain. Add dough ingredients to breadmaker. Select Dough cycle. When cycle is complete, take dough out and roll out on a floured board into a rectangle. Brush dough with melted butter. Combine filling ingredients. Sprinkle dough with this mixture. Roll jellyroll fashion, starting with long edge. Seal edges, slice into 5-20 rolls, depending on the size of your recipe. Place cut side down onto sprayed baking sheet. Cover and let rise in a warm place until doubled (*at least one hour, preferably two hours*). Bake at 350 degrees for 20-25 minutes. Brush with melted butter, then drizzle with icing.

Variation: Omit nuts and add 1/4-1/2 c. chocolate chips.

Breadmixer Bread Techeques (4-5 Loaves)

Instructions for use are included with individual breadmixers. Most are similar, but the kneading times may vary. Some breadmixers mix and knead in only 2-4 minutes; some take as long as 10-12 minutes. Be sure to follow the mixing and kneading time for your machine.

>   12-15 c. whole wheat flour
>   2 1/2 Tb. instant yeast
>   1/4 c. oil
>   2 Tb. salt
>   5 1/4 c. warm water
>   1/2 c. honey

Optional Ingredients

Any of the compinations listed below may be added to your bread.

A. 1/2 c. gluten flour
>   2-3 T. Dough Enhancer, or 60 mg. ascorbic acid
B. 1/2 c. whey powder
>   1-2 c. molasses (omit honey)
>   2 T. liquid lecithin (in place of 2 T. oil called for in recipe)
C. 3-4 eggs (decrease liquid by 1/4 c. for each egg)
D. 1 c. dry milk powder (blend in with the 5 1/4 c. warm water, scald, then cool to lukewarm)
E. 1 cup mashed potatoes

1. Mill aproximately 10-11 c. wheat. As it is milling, combine the warm water or milk, oil, honey, and salt in mixing bowl.

2. Add 7 c. wheat flour, instant yeast (or the disolved regular yeast), and any optional ingredients into the first mixture.

3. Mix together on low speed for about 1 minute. Continue adding flour as the machine mixes on low speed (5-6 cups at first, then 1/2 c. at a time) until the dough is the desired consistency. The dough should be pliable, but not too sticky or too dry.

4. Continue mixing dough on high speed, following mixer manufacturer's directions, until gluten is developed.

5. If desired, the dough may be turned out into a sprayed bowl, covered, and allowed to rise until double. After dough has doubled in size, punch down, place on lightly sprayed counter, and shape into loaves.

6. Step 5 above may be omitted, and the dough turned out onto a lightly sprayed counter, kneaded slightly, and divided into loaves or other shapes.

7. Place formed loaves into sprayed pans. Let rise in warm place, covered with warm, damp towel, until double in size.

8. Bake loaves in a pre-heated oven at 400 degrees for 10 minutes. Turn oven to 350 degrees and continue baking for 25-30 minutes. Cover with aluminum foil the last 20 minutes, if necessary, to prevent excess browning.

BREADMIXER BREAD TECHNIQUES (6-7 LOAVES)

If you have a breadmixer that holds up to 12 pounds of dough, the recipe that follows will utilize the large capacity of the bowl.

18-22 c. whole wheat flour
1/3 c. oil
3/4 c. honey
2 1/2 Tb. salt
3 Tb. instant yeast or
4 Tb. regular yeast, dissolved in 1/2 c. of the warm water used in the recipe
7 1/2 c. warm water

OPTIONAL INGREDIENTS
Any of the combinations listed below may be added to your bread.

A. 1/2 c. gluten flour

Up to 4 eggs (decrease liquid by 1/4 c. for each egg)

B. 1-2 c. whey

1/4 c. molasses

3 T. lecithin (in place of 3 T. oil called for in recipe)

C. 75 mg. ascorbic acid or 4 T. dough enhancer

D. 1 1/4 c. dry milk powder (blend in with the 7 c. warm water, scald, then cool to lukewarm)

E. 1 1/4 c. mashed potatoes

1. Mill approximately 12-15 c. wheat. As it is milling, add the warm water or milk, fat, honey, and salt together in mixing bowl.

2. Add 10 c. wheat flour, instant yeast (or the dissolved regular yeast), and any optional ingredients into the first mixture.

3. Mix together on low speed as more flour is added, 1 cup at a time, until the dough reaches the desired consistency.

4. Continue mixing dough on high speed, following mixer manufacturer's directions, until gluten is developed.

5. Place dough on a lightly sprayed counter, knead slightly, then shape into loaves or other shapes.

(5).Dough may be turned out into a sprayed bowl, covered, and allowed to rise until double. After dough has doubled in size, punch down, place on lightly sprayed counter, and shape into loaves.

6. Place formed loaves into sprayed pans. Let rise in warm place, covered with warm, damp towel, until double in size.

7. Bake loaves in pre-heated oven at 400 degrees for 10 minutes. Turn oven to 350 degrees and continue baking for 25-30 minutes. Cover with aluminum foil the last 20 minutes, if necessary, to prevent excess browning.

FRENCH BREAD

1. Use any of the bread recipes given, omitting oil and sweetener. After the dough is completely kneaded, place dough into a lightly sprayed bowl, cover, and allow to rise until double.

2. Punch down carefully, then let rest for 10 minutes.

Divide dough into 3 cup portions.

3. For round loaves, pound dough into a tight ball. Place in center of lightly sprayed pan that has been sprinkled with corn meal.

4. For oblong loaves, roll each portion to an 8" x 16" rectangle. Roll up the short way, creating a long roll. Use a rolling pin to slightly flatten the loaf. Place on greased pan that has been lightly sprinkled with corn meal.

5. For a twisted oblong loaf, follow step 4 above. After rolling the dough into an oblong shape, let it rest 5-10 minutes. Twist the dough two full turns, then place on pan as directed above.

6. Slash each loaf on the top with a sharp serrated knife. Make sure that the slashes cut into the loaves at a diagonal angle, not straight down.

7. Cover the loaves with a warm, damp towel and allow to rise in a warm place until double.

8. Bake in a preheated oven at 425 degrees for 10 minutes. Lower oven temperature to 350 degrees for remaining 25 minutes.

9. The secret to good French bread is in the baking. Steam creates a thick, lightly browned, chewy crust. To create steam in the oven, spray each loaf of bread with water from a spray bottle 3-4 times during the first 10 minutes of baking.

10. Another way to create steam is to place a pan of hot water in the oven below the baking French bread. This is not as effective as commercial methods, but it may be the best solution for you.

PITA BREAD

1. Make any of the bread recipes given, omitting oil. Take care to ensure that your dough is a soft dough, and not dry and hard.

2. Allow to rest for 10 minutes. Break out 1/2 cup size portions of dough. Form balls, cover with clean towel, and let stand 15 minutes.

3. Preheat oven to 475 degrees. The oven must be completely warmed, because this creates the pocket.

4. Roll each ball to 1/2 inch thickness (roll out on counter that has been lightly floured). Place on ungreased cookie sheet that has been sprinkled with 1/4 c. cornmeal. If you are making a large recipe, place on counter that is sprinkled with cornmeal. When you are ready to bake, move gently with fingers to cornmeal-covered cookie sheet.

5. Allow to rise for a half hour.

6. Bake on lowest rack of oven for 5-10 minutes or until puffed up and turning brown.

7. Remove from oven and allow to cool completely. Store in closed plastic bags in refrigerator, or freeze for longer storage.

PITA BREAD HELPFUL HINTS

A. The basic plan in making pita bread is to get steam to puff up inside the bread before the bread bakes. This is why you need a soft, moist dough with no fat in it. Also, this is why the bread is baked at a very high temperature at the bottom of the oven.

B. If your bread is burning on the bottom before it can puff up, try putting your cookie sheet on the next-to-bottom shelf of the oven with the oven turned up to 500 degrees F.

C. Thick cookie sheets may not allow heat to penetrate quickly enough to the pita bread. This will cause the bread to cook before it has a chance to puff up. Thin cookie sheets generally work better for this type of bread.

Rolls, Buns, and Breadsticks Techniques

Cinnamon Rolls

1. Use any of the bread recipes above, adding an extra 1/2 c. sugar, if desired, to make a sweeter dough.

2. On a lightly sprayed counter, roll 6 cups of dough into a 12"x16" rectangle. Spread dough with 6 Tb. melted butter or margarine.

3. Spread with a mixture of 1 c. white or brown sugar and 1 tsp. cinnamon.

4. Sprinkle with 1 c. coarsely chopped walnuts or pecans (1 c. raisins is optional).

5. Roll up and seal ends. Use dental floss or heavy thread to cut the dough into 1 1/2 inch wide rolls. Flatten the cinnamon rolls slightly onto 2 or 3 sprayed cookie sheets.

6. Cover and let rise 45-60 minutes. Bake in preheated oven at 375 degrees for 20-25 minutes. Frost when cool.

Frosting for Cinnamon Rolls

4 c. powdered sugar
6 Tb. butter or margarine
1 tsp. vanilla
3-6 Tb. milk or cream

Mix sugar, butter, and vanilla together. Add milk or cream gradually until frosting is smooth and spreads easily.

Variations:

Substitute 1/2-1 tsp. almond or maple flavoring for the vanilla.

Substitute 3 oz. cream cheese for 3 Tb. of the butter or margarine.

Add 1/2 tsp. coconut flavoring to frosting. Sprinkle frosted cinnamon rolls with shredded coconut.

Dinner Rolls

1. Use any of the above recipes, substituting 3 eggs for 3/4 cup of liquid called for in the recipe.

2. Place dough on lightly sprayed counter and break out 1/2 c. size pieces of dough. Divide each in half again, pound into a small ball, and place on a greased cookie sheet. An average size cookie sheet holds 20-24 dinner rolls.

3. Crescent rolls may be formed by rolling 2 c. dough into a 12 inch circle. Cut dough into pie-shaped pieces and brush with melted butter if desired. Roll up, beginning with large end. Curve into crescents and place on a sprayed cookie sheet.

4. Cover and let rise in warm place until double. Bake in preheated oven at 375 degrees for 20 minutes.

Bread Sticks

1. Use any of the bread recipes given. Roll 2 c. dough to 1/2 inch thickness. Cut strips of dough 1-2 inches wide, and 6-8 inches long.

2. If desired, spread with melted butter or beaten egg white. Sprinkle with parmesan cheese or sesame seeds.

3. Twist bread sticks and lay on sprayed cookie sheet.

4. Cover and allow to rise 30-45 minutes. Bake in pre-heated oven at 375 degrees for 15 minutes.

Hamburger Buns

1. Using any of the basic bread recipes given, roll desired amount of dough to 3/4 inch thickness. Cut circles of desired size and transfer to sprayed cookie sheet. (A wide-mouth thermos lid works well, or wide-mouth gallon lid).

2. If desired, brush tops with beaten egg white and

sprinkle with sesame seeds.

3. Cover and allow to rise until double. Bake in pre-heated oven at 375 degrees for 20-25 minutes.

HOT DOG OR DELI BUNS

1. Using any of the bread recipes given, roll desired amount of dough to 1/2 inch thickness. Cut circles of desired size Fold circle in half, and stretch to elongate. (I found a thin metal cookie cutter, which I reshaped to make a hot dog-shaped bun).

2. Place on sprayed cookie sheet. If desired, brush tops with beaten egg white and sprinkle with sesame seeds.

3. Cover and allow to rise until double. Bake in pre-heated oven at 375 degrees for 23 minutes.

CHAPTER THREE

WHEAT BREAD RECIPES

BREADMIXER RECIPES

The recipes in this section make more than one loaf of bread. For this reason, they are separated from the breadmaker recipes. However, as you gain more experience in breadmaking, you may wish to make some of these recipes in a breadmaker. Try cutting the ingredients in halves, or fourths. Be sure to use the principles of whole wheat breadmaking, and follow the specific instructions for your breadmaker.

You may also make any of the following recipes by hand.

APPLESAUCE BREAD
(3-4 LOAVES)

This is a healthy bread calling for applesauce instead of oil. It tastes great when spread with apple butter.

2 c. warm water or apple juice
2 c. applesauce
1/2 c. sugar
1 T. salt
2 T. instant yeast
8-11 c. wheat flour
1/3 c. gluten flour

Measure warm water or apple juice into mixing bowl. Add applesauce, sugar, salt, and 7 cups wheat flour. Mix ingredients together on low speed. After 1 minute, add gluten flour and yeast. Increase mixer speed while adding remaining flour, 1/2 c. at a time until dough pulls away from sides of bowl. Knead until gluten is fully developed.

Turn dough out onto sprayed counter. Mold dough into loaves, place in sprayed bread pans, cover, and let rise until double. Bake in preheated oven at 400 degrees for 10 minutes. Lower oven temperature to 350 degrees and continue baking for 25-30 minutes. Cover loaves with aluminum foil the last 15 minutes to prevent excess browning.

BUCKWHEAT BREAD
(4-5 LOAVES)

5 c. warm water
2 T. instant yeast
2 T. salt
1/2 c. brown sugar
2 T. lecithin
2 T. oil
2/3 c. gluten flour
100 mg. ascorbic acid
2 c. buckwheat flour
11-13 c. wheat flour
2 t. maple flavoring (opt.)

Mill 2 c. hulled buckwheat, then measure 2 c. buckwheat flour. Set aside. Mill 8-10 c. wheat. Add buckwheat flour to 5 c. warm water in mixer bowl. Add salt, sugar, lecithin and oil mixed together, and 7 c. wheat flour. Begin mixing on low speed while adding yeast, 2-4 more c. wheat flour, ascorbic acid, and gluten flour. After 1 minute, increase mixer speed while adding more wheat flour, 1/2 c. at a time until dough pulls away from sides of bowl. Knead dough until gluten is developed.

Turn dough out onto sprayed counter. Mold into loaves, place in sprayed pans, cover, and let rise until double.

Bake in preheated oven at 400 degrees for 10 minutes. Turn heat down to 350 degrees and continue baking for 20-25 minutes until loaves are done.

PINTO BEAN BREAD
(4-5 LOAVES)

5 1/4 c. warm water
14-17 c. wheat flour
2 c. cooked, mashed pinto beans*
2 T. salt
2 T. lecithin
2 T. oil
1/2 c. honey

2 1/2 T. instant yeast
1/2 c. gluten flour
75 mg. ascorbic acid

Measure warm water in mixing bowl. Add pinto beans, salt, lecithin mixed with oil, honey, and 7 cups flour. Slowly blend ingredients together on low speed while adding 2 more cups flour, instant yeast, and gluten flour. Increase mixing speed while adding more flour, 1/2 c. at a time until dough pulls completely away from sides of mixing bowl. Knead until gluten is fully developed.

Turn dough out onto lightly sprayed counter. Spray hands lightly. Form dough into loaves, place in sprayed pans, cover, and let rise until double. Bake in preheated oven at 400 degrees for 10 minutes. Lower oven temperature to 350 degrees and continue baking for 25-30 minutes. Cover loaves with aluminum foil during last 15 minutes to prevent excess browning.

Pinto bean bread has a very light texture. It goes well with hearty corn chowder.

*For quick pinto beans, mill 1 1/2 c. pinto beans in your mill. Stir it into 3 c. boiling water. Cover and cook over low heat for 5-6 minutes. Remove from heat and allow to cool. Measure out 2 cups for bread.

Pumpernickel Bread
(3-4 Loaves)

4 1/2 c. warm water
1/2 c. molasses
1 1/2 T. lecithin
1 1/2 T. oil
2 T. salt
2 1/2 T. cocoa powder
3 T. instant yeast
2 T. caraway seed
1 1/2 c. rye flour
8-10 c. wheat flour
1/2 c. gluten flour

Measure water, molasses, lecithin and oil mixed together, salt, cocoa, caraway seed, and rye flour into mixing bowl.

Begin mixing on low speed while adding 6-7 cups

wheat flour. Add gluten flour and yeast. Increase mixer speed, adding remaining flour 1/2 cup at a time until dough pulls away from sides of mixing bowl. Knead until gluten is fully developed.

Turn dough out onto lightly sprayed counter. Form into 3 rounds of dough, pounding each with your fist into a tight, smooth ball. Place each on a sprayed cookie sheet. Slash the top of each with a sharp knife. Cover and let rise until double. Bake in a preheated oven at 350 degrees until done.

SESAME SEED BREAD
(3-4 LOAVES)

4 c. warm water
1/2 c. honey
1 c. powdered whey
1 T. salt
3 eggs
2 1/2 T. oil
2 T. instant yeast
1 c. mashed potatoes (opt.)

1/2 c. gluten flour
1/2 c. sesame seeds
9-12 c. wheat flour

1 beaten egg white
2-3 T. sesame seeds

Measure warm water, honey, whey, salt, eggs, and oil into mixing bowl. Add mashed potatoes, 5 c. flour, yeast, and 1/2 c. sesame seeds. Mix together on low speed. Add 3 more cups flour, turn mixer to medium speed, and add flour 1/2 c. at a time until dough pulls away from sides of mixing bowl. Knead until gluten is developed.

Turn dough out onto lightly oiled or sprayed counter and form into loaves. Spray loaf pans with PAM™, then sprinkle 1 1/2 teaspoons of sesame seeds into the bottom of each loaf pan. Place formed loaves in pans, on top of sesame seeds. Brush tops of loaves with egg white, then sprinkle 1 teaspoon sesame seeds over the top of each loaf. The sesame seeds will adhere to the egg white. Cover lightly with a dry cloth and let rise until double.

Bake in a preheated oven at 400 degrees F. for 10 minutes. Turn oven down to 350 degrees and continue baking for 25-30 minutes. Remove from oven and cool on racks.

Sunflower Seed Bread
(4-5 Loaves)

5 1/2 c. warm water
1/4 c. molasses
1 1/2 T. salt
2 T. oil
2 T. liquid lecithin
100 mg. ascorbic acid
2 c. oats, coarsely ground in blender
2/3 c. gluten flour
9-12 c. whole wheat flour
1 1/2 c. sunflower seeds
2 1/2 T. instant yeast

Measure warm water, molasses, salt, oil mixed with lecithin, and ascorbic acid into mixing bowl. Add oats, sunflower seeds, 5 c. wheat flour, gluten flour, and then the instant yeast. Mix together on low speed, then add 5 more cups flour. Increase speed to medium, then add flour 1/2 c. at a time until dough pulls away from the sides of the bowl. Knead until gluten is developed.

Turn dough out onto slightly oiled or sprayed counter. Form into loaves, place in sprayed pans, cover, and let rise until double. Bake in preheated oven at 400 degrees F. for 10 minutes. Reduce heat to 350 degrees and bake 25-30 minutes longer. Remove from oven and cool on racks.

Wheat-Corn Bread
(4-5 Loaves)

This bread resembles the early American Anadama Bread. Corn flour is used instead of cornmeal, giving a finer texture to the bread.

5 1/2 c. warm water
13-16 c. whole wheat flour
2 1/2 T. instant yeast
1/4 c. molasses
2 T. honey

2 T. lecithin
2 T. oil
2 T. salt
3 c. corn meal or corn flour
1/2 c. gluten flour

Measure water, molasses, honey, oil and lecithin mixed together, salt, and corn flour to mixing bowl. Add 7 cups wheat flour. Turn breadmixer to low speed. While mixing, add 1/2 c. gluten flour and instant yeast. After 1 minute, increase speed of breadmixer and gradually add remaining wheat flour, 1/2-1 cup at a time until dough pulls away from sides of bowl. Continue kneading until gluten is fully developed.

Turn dough out onto a lightly sprayed counter. Shape into loaves, place in sprayed bread pans, cover and let rise until double. Bake in preheated oven at 400 degrees for 10 minutes. Turn oven to 350 degrees and continue baking for 25-30 minutes or until done. Cover loaves with aluminum foil the last 20 minutes to prevent excess browning.

This bread has a delicate corn flavor, and is delicious with ham and bean stew.

WHOLE WHEAT PIZZA CRUST
(TWO 12" CRUSTS)

2 1/2 c. warm water
1 T. instant yeast
2 t. sugar
1/2 c. whey
1 1/2 t. Italian Seasoning
5-6 c. wheat flour
1 T. salt
1/4 c. mashed potatoes

Dissolve yeast in 1/2 c. warm water. Meanwhile, measure into breadmixer bowl 2 c. warm water, 2 t. sugar, whey, Italian Seasoning, and mashed potatoes. Add 3 c. whole wheat flour and mix on low speed for 1 minute. Add yeast, and 2 more cups flour. Continue mixing on a medium speed as you add flour, 1/4 c. at a time until dough is firm, but not stiff. Knead according to breadmixer instructions until gluten is fully developed.

Remove dough from mixer and let rest for 15 minutes on lightly sprayed surface. For very light pizza crust, allow dough to rise until double in size (cover with towel). Punch down, divide dough in half, then let rest 10 minutes. Spray two 12" pizza pans with PAM™.

After dough has rested, begin gently stretching one portion of dough into a 12" circle. Place your hands under the small circle of dough, palms down (dough will be resting on the backs of your hands). Pull your hands apart under the dough (keeping fingers extended), gently stretching the dough. You may want to try gently tossing the dough into the air from the backs of your hands, causing it to twirl in the air. Let it come back down on the backs of your hands. Repeat until dough is basically the size of the pizza pan. Place dough on pan, gently stretching it to fit. Do not roll dough with a pizza roller; it flattens all the air bubbles that were just created by all the twirling. Repeat with the other portion of dough.

Allow dough to rise until double. Preheat oven to 450 degrees F. Bake pizza crust for 6 minutes. Remove from oven and spread with desired toppings. Return to oven and bake 7-8 more minutes until cheese melts.

BREADMAKER RECIPES (SINGLE LOAVES)

The recipes that follow have been formulated especially for breadmakers. However, any of them may be made in any breadmixer or hand-kneaded batch of bread. The recipes may also be doubled or tripled so that more than one loaf can be made at a time. Experiment and find your favorite recipes. You'll enjoy the variety of breads that you'll be able to create!

ALMOND-OAT BREAD

	Large	Medium	Small
Lukewarm Water	1 1/2 c.	1 1/8 c.	3/4 c.
Honey	3 T.	2 1/4 T.	1 1/2 T.
Oats	3/4 c.	1/2 c.	1/4 c.
Salt	2 t.	1 1/2 t.	1 t.
Powdered Milk	1/4 c.	3 T.	2 T.

Gluten Flour	3 T.	2 1/4 T.	1 1/2 T.
Wheat Flour	3 1/4 c.	2 1/2 c.	1 3/4 c.
Instant Yeast	1 T.	2 1/4 t.	1 1/2 t.
Butter	2 1/2 T.	2 T.	1 1/4 T.
Almond Flavor	1 T.	2 1/4 t.	1 1/2 t.

Measure lukewarm water into breadmaker, followed by remaining ingredients. Add the yeast last, then program the breadmaker for raisin bread. At the beep (or near the end of the second knead cycle), add:

Slivered Almond	3/4 c.	1/2 c.	6 T.

If desired, omit the almonds, then program the breadmaker for regular bread.

BUTTERMILK CHEESE BREAD

	Large	Medium	Small
Buttermilk	1 c.	3/4 c.	1/2 c.
Warm Water	1/4 c.	3 T.	2 T.
Grated Cheese (X-sharp)	1 c.	3/4 c.	1/2 c.

Sugar	1 T.	2 1/4 t.	1 1/2 t.
Salt	1 t.	3/4 t.	1/2 t.
Wheat Flour	2 7/8 c.	2 1/8 c.	1 1/2 c.
Baking Soda	1 t.	3/4 t.	1/2 t.
Gluten Flour	3 T.	2 1/4 T.	1 1/2 T.
Instant Yeast	2 t.	1 1/2 t.	1 t.

Measure all ingredients into the Breadmaker in the order given.

Select the wheat bread setting (or white bread if there is no option), then start the machine.

Instant Yeast	2 t.	1 1/2 t.	1 t.
Raisins (opt.)	2/3 c.	1/2 c.	1/3 c.

Measure ingredients into breadmaker in order given. If you use raisins in your recipe, select the raisin bread cycle. If you do not use raisins, select the wheat bread setting (or white if you do not have a wheat bread setting), then start the machine.

BUTTERMILK WHEAT BREAD

	Large	Medium	Small
Buttermilk	1 1/2 c.	1 c.	3/4 c.
Butter	1 T.	2 t.	1 1/2 t.
Wheat Flour	3 1/4 c.	2 3/8 c.	1 3/4 c.
Gluten Flour	3 T.	2 T	1 T.
Salt	1 1/2 t.	1 t.	3/4 t.
Baking Soda	1 1/2 t.	1 t.	3/4 t.
Caraway Seeds	3 T.	2 1/4 T.	1 1/2 T.

CHEDDAR CHEESE BREAD

	Large	Medium	Small
Lukewarm Water	1 1/3 c.	1 c.	2/3 c.
Sugar	2 T.	1 1/2 T.	1 T.
Powdered Milk	1/3 c.	3 2/3 T.	2 1/2 T.
Salt	1 1/2 t.	1 1/4 t.	3/4 t.
Eggs	2	1	1
Butter	2 T.	1 1/2 T.	1 T.
Wheat Flour	4 c.	3 c.	2 c.
Gluten Flour	3 T.	2 1/4 T.	1 1/2 T.

Instant Yeast	2 1/2 t.	2 t.	1 1/4 t.
Black Pepper (Opt.)	1 t.	3/4 t.	1/2 t.

Butter	1 T.	3/4 T.	1/2 T.
Salt	1 1/2 t.	1 t.	3/4 t.
Molasses	1/3 c.	4 T.	2 3/4 T.
Wheat Flour	3 3/8 c.	2 1/2 c.	1 3/4 c.
Gluten Flour	2 T.	1 1/2 T.	1 T.
Instant Yeast	2 t.	1 1/2 t.	1 t.

Measure liquid ingredients into breadmaker (including slightly beaten eggs). Measure in the dry ingredients next, ending with yeast. Program breadmaker to make raisin bread. Begin cycle, then prepare cheese mixture as follows:

Grated Cheddar Cheese	1 c.	3/4 c.	1/2 c.
Wheat Flour	2 T.	1 1/2 T.	1 T.

Place flour in plastic bag. Add grated cheese and shake bag, coating cheese with flour. Sift remaining flour out, then add to bread dough when the breadmaker beeps. If your machine has no raisin bread cycle, add the cheese during the last two minutes of the second knead cycle.

Place cornmeal into bowl. Carefully stir boiling water into cornmeal until it is smooth. Let cool for about 30 minutes. Pour into breadmaker, followed by other ingredients in the order given. Select the wheat bread setting (or white if you have no wheat bread option), then start the machine. Colonial Bread is delicious when served with Ham and Bean Soup.

CRACKED WHEAT BREAD

	Large	Medium	Small
Boiling Water	1/2 c.	3/8 c.	1/4 c.
Cracked Wheat	1/2 c.	3/8 c.	1/4 c.
Lecithin	2 T.	1 1/2 T.	1 T.
Evaporated Milk	12 oz.	1 1/8 c.	6 oz.

COLONIAL BREAD

	Large	Medium	Small
Boiling Water	1 1/2 c.	1 1/8 c.	3/4 c.
Corn Meal	1/3 c.	4 T.	2 3/4 T.

Honey	3 T.	2 1/4 T.	1 1/2 T.
Salt	1 1/2 t.	2 1/8 t.	3/4 t.
Wheat Flour	3 5/8 c.	2 3/4 c.	1 7/8 c.
Gluten Flour	2 T.	1 1/2 T.	1 T.
Ginger	1/8 t.	pinch	pinch
Instant Yeast	2 t.	1 1/2 t.	1 t.

Cover the 1/2 c. cracked wheat (crack your own in your blender, or purchase it in a health food store) with boiling water in a small bowl. When it is cool, place it in the breadmaker, followed by the other ingredients in the order given. Select the wheat bread setting (or white if you have no wheat bread option), then start the machine.

French Bread

	Large	Medium	Small
Hot Water	1 c.	3/4 c.	1/2 c.
Butter	2 T.	1 1/2 T.	1 T.
Salt	1 t.	3/4 t.	1/2 t.
Sugar	2 T.	1 1/2 T.	1 T.
Wheat Flour	3 c.	2 1/4 c.	1 1/2 c.

Gluten Flour	2 T.	1 1/2 T.	1 T.
Instant Yeast	2 t.	1 1/2 t.	1 t.
Egg Whites	2	1	1

Whip egg whites until stiff and set aside. Place other ingredients in breadmaker in order given. Start machine on French Bread setting. When all ingredients are moistened, add egg whites.

Golden Egg Bread

	Large	Medium	Small
Warm Water	3/4 c.	1/2 c.	3/8 c.
Oil	2 T.	1 1/2 T.	1 T.
Eggs	2	1	1
Sugar	4 T.	3 T.	2 T.
Salt	1 1/2 t.	1 1/8 t.	3/4 t.
Wheat Flour	2 7/8 c.	2 1/4 c.	1 1/2 c.
Gluten Flour	2 T.	1 1/2 T.	1 T.
Instant Yeast	2 t.	1 1/2 t.	1 t.

This bread turns out better if you use white wheat flour.

Add all ingredients to your breadmaker in the order given. Select the white or wheat bread setting, depending on which breadmaker you have.

Add all ingredients to the breadmaker in the order given. Select the wheat bread setting (or white bread if you have no wheat bread option), then start the machine.

GRAHAM BREAD

Graham flour, used to make great crackers, is available in health food stores. It gives a delicious taste to whole wheat bread.

	Large	Medium	Small
Warm Water	1 1/4 c.	1 c.	5/8 c.
Butter	1 T.	3/4 T.	1/2 T.
Honey	1 T.	3/4 T.	1/2 T.
Salt	1 1/2 t.	1 1/8 t.	3/4 t.
Dry Milk	1/4 c.	3 T.	2 T.
Graham Flour	2 c.	1 1/2 c.	1 c.
Wheat Flour	1 7/8 c.	1 1/2 c.	1 c.
Gluten Flour	2 T.	1 1/2 T.	1 T.
Instant Yeast	2 t.	1 1/2 t.	1 t.

GRANOLA BREAD

	Large	Medium	Small
Warm Water	3/4 c.	3/8 c.	1/4 c.
Buttermilk	1/2 c.	3/8 c.	1/4 c.
Butter	2 T.	1 1/2 T.	1 T.
Honey	2 T.	1 1/2 T.	1 T.
Egg	1	1	1
Sugar	13/4 t.	1 t.	3/4 t.
Salt	3/4 t.	1/2 t.	3/8 t.
Granola	1 c.	3/4 c.	1/2 c.
Wheat Flour	2 5/8 c.	2 1/8 c.	1 3/8 c.
Gluten Flour	2 T.	1 1/2 T.	1 T.
Instant Yeast	2 t.	1 1/2 t.	1 t.

Grind the granola in a blender until fine. Add all the ingredients to the breadmaker in the order given. Select the wheat bread setting (or white if you have no wheat bread option), then start the machine.

Hawaiian Coconut Bread

	Large	Medium	Small
Warm Water	1/4 c.	3 T.	2 T.
Pineapple Juice	1/2 c.	1/3 c.	1/4 c.
Crushed Pineapple	1/2 c.	1/3 c.	1/4 c.
Whole Macadamia Nuts or Almonds	3/4 c.	1/2 c.	3/8 c.
Shredded Coconut	3/4 c.	1/2 c.	3/8 c.
Butter	2 T.	1 1/2 T.	1 T.
Egg	1	1	1
Dry Milk Powder	1/4 c.	3 T.	2 T.
Sugar	1 T.	2 t.	1 1/2 t.
Salt	2 t.	1 1/2 t.	1 t.
Wheat Flour	2 7/8 c.	2 1/8 c.	1 1/2
Gluten Flour	2 T.	1 1/2 T.	1 T.

| Instant Yeast | 2 t. | 1 1/2 t. | 1 t. |

Drain crushed pineapple, reserving liquid (use 1/2 c. in recipe). Add all ingredients in the order given. Select the wheat bread setting (or white if you have no wheat bread option), then start the machine.

Healthy (Caraway) Seed Bread

	Large	Medium	Small
Egg	1	1	1
Honey	4 T.	3 T.	2 T.
Oil	1 T.	3/4 T.	1/2 T.
Warm Milk	1/3 c.	2 T.	1 1/2 T.
Warm Water	1 c.	3/4 c.	1/2 c.
Caraway Seeds	2 T.	1 1/2 T.	1 T.
Chopped Nuts	1/4 c.	3 T.	2 T.
Corn Flour	1/2 c.	3/8 c.	1/4 c.
Rye Flour	2/3 c.	1/2 c.	1/3 c.
Sugar	1 T.	2 t.	1 1/2 T.
Wheat Flour	2 3/4 c.	2 1/8 c.	1 1/2 c.

Gluten Flour	3 T.	2 1/4 T.	1 1/2 T.
Instant Yeast	2 t.	1 1/2 t.	1 t.

Measure ingredients into breadmaker in order given. Select the wheat bread setting (use the white bread setting if you have no wheat bread option), then start the machine.

ITALIAN BREAD

	Large	Medium	Small
Warm Water	1 1/2 c.	1 1/8 c.	3/4 c.
Olive Oil	1 T.	3/4 T.	1/2 T.
Italian Seasoning	1 t.	3/4 t.	1/2 t.
Parmesan Cheese	1/3 c.	1/4 c.	2 1/2 T.
Garlic Salt	1 t.	3/4 t.	1/2 t.
Sugar	1 T.	3/4 T.	1/2 T.
Wheat Flour	2 7/8 c.	2 1/8 c.	1 1/2 c.
Gluten Flour	2 T.	1 1/2 T.	1 T.
Instant Yeast	2 t.	1 1/2 t.	1 t.

Measure all ingredients into breadmaker in the order given. Select the wheat bread setting (or white if you have no wheat bread option), then start the machine.

LEMON POPPY SEED BREAD

	Large	Medium	Small
Lukewarm Water	1 1/3 c.	1 c.	2/3 c.
Lemon Juice	3 T.	2 1/4 T.	1 1/2 T.
Grated Lemon Peel	1 T.	2 1/4 t.	1 1/2 t.
Butter	2 T.	1 1/2 T.	1 T.
Salt	2 t.	1 1/2 t.	1 t.
Sugar	1/2 c.	1/3 c.	1/4 c.
Instant Powdered Milk	1/2 c.	1/3 c.	1/4 c.
Poppy Seeds	1 T.	3/4 T.	1/2 T.
Wheat Flour	4 c.	3 c.	2 c.
Gluten Flour	3 T.	2 1/4 T.	1 1/2 T.
Instant Yeast	1 T.	2 t.	1 1/2 t.

The delicate lemon flavor of this bread is more noticeable when the wheat flour is milled from white wheat, and not red wheat. If you use red wheat, you may want to increase the sugar by 1 T., and the lemon peel by 1/2 tsp.

Measure all the ingredients into the breadmaker, beginning with the liquids, and ending with the instant yeast. Program the breadmaker for basic white bread, then start the machine. You may also want to use the lightest crust setting.

Maple Oatmeal Bread

	Large	Medium	Small
Warm Water	1 3/8 c.	1 c.	5/8 c.
Oil	1 T.	2 t.	1 1/2 t.
Maple Syrup	1/3 c.	3 1/2 T.	2 T.
Maple Flavoring	1 t.	3/4 t.	1/2 t.
Salt	1 t.	3/4 t.	1/2 t.
Oats	1 c.	3/4 c.	1/2 c.
Wheat Flour	2 7/8 c.	2 1/8 c.	1 1/2 c.
Gluten Flour	2 T.	1 1/2 T.	1 T.
Instant Yeast	2 t.	1 1/2 t.	1 t.

Put all ingredients into breadmaker in the order listed. Select the wheat bread setting (or white bread if you have no wheat bread option), then start the machine.

Maple-Peacan Bread

	Large	Medium	Small
Lukewarm Water	1 1/2 c.	1 c.	3/4 c.
Brown Sugar	1/2 c.	6 T.	1/4 c.
Instant Yeast	2 1/2 t.	2 t.	1 1/4 t.
Maple Flavoring	1 1/2 t.	1 t.	3/4 t.
Salt	1 1/2 t.	1 t.	3/4 t.
Butter	2 T.	1 1/2 T.	1 T.
Wheat Flour	3 3/4 c.	2 3/4 c.	1 3/4 c.
Gluten Flour	3 T.	2 1/4 T.	1 1/2 T.

Measure water, then other ingredients into breadmaker, adding yeast last. Program the breadmaker for raisin bread. At the beep, add:

	Large	Medium	Small
Chopped Pecans	2/3 c.	1/2 c.	1/3 c.

If your machine has no raisin bread cycle, add pecans during the last minute or two of the second kneading.

OAT BREAD

	Large	Medium	Small
Warm Water	1 1/2 c.	1 1/8 c.	3/4 c.
Butter	1 T.	3/4 T.	1/2 T.
Salt	1 t.	3/4 t.	1/2 t.
Sugar	1 T.	3/4 T.	1/2 T.
Rolled Oats	1 c.	3/4 c.	1/2 c.
Wheat Flour	2 7/8 c.	2 1/8 c.	1 1/2 c.
Gluten Flour	2 T.	1 1/2 T.	1 T.
Instant Yeast	1 1/2 t.	1 1/8 t.	3/4 t.

Grind rolled oats in a blender until fine. Add all ingredients to the breadmaker in the order given. Select the wheat bread setting (or white if you have no wheat bread option), then start the machine.

OAT BRAN APPLE BREAD

	Large	Medium	Small
Warm Apple Juice	1 1/2 c.	1 1/8 c.	3/4 c.
Peeled Grated Apples	2 c.	1 1/2 c.	1 c.
Egg Whites	2	1	1
Honey	2 T.	1 1/2 T.	1 T.
Oil	1 T.	2 1/4 t.	1 1/2 t.
Cinnamon	1 t.	3/4 t.	1/2 t.
Salt	1 1/2 t.	1 t.	3/4 t.
Rolled Oats	1 c.	3/4 c.	1/2 c.
Oat Bran	2 1/4 c.	1 3/4 c.	1 1/8 c.
Wheat Flour	3 1/4 c.	2 3/8 c.	1 5/8 c.
Gluten Flour	4 T.	3 T.	2 T.
Instant Yeast	2 t.	1 1/2 t.	1 t.

Measure ingredients into breadmaker in order given. The recipe is very large, and the pan will be very full. The bread will not rise very much, but the finished loaf will still be very tall. Select the white or wheat bread setting (wheat if your machine has the option), then push the start button.

Oat Bran Banana Bread

	Large	Medium	Small
Warm Water	2 1/8 c.	1 1/2 c.	1 c.
Sliced Bananas	2	1 1/2	1
Egg Whites	2	1	1
Honey	2 T.	1 1/2 T.	1 T.
Oil	2 T.	2 T.	1 T.
Salt	1 t.	3/4 t.	1/2 t.
Oat Bran	2 1/4 c.	1 3/4 c.	1 1/8 c.
Rolled Oats	1 c.	3/4 c.	1/2 c.
Wheat Flour	3 1/4 c.	2 1/2 c.	1 5/8 c.
Gluten Flour	4 T.	3 T.	2 T.
Instant Yeast	2 t.	1 1/2 t.	1 t.

Measure ingredients into breadmaker in order given. This recipe is large, and the dough will almost fill the pan. However, the bread will not rise very much. Select the wheat bread setting (or white if there is no option for wheat), then start the machine.

Oat Bran Bread

	Large	Medium	Small
Lukewarm Water	1 1/2 c.	1 c.	3/4 c.
Wheat Flour	3 1/4 c.	2 3/8 c.	1 3/4 c.
Gluten Flour	3 T.	2 1/4 T.	1 1/2 T.
Molasses	2 T.	1 1/2 T.	1 T.
Oat Bran	1/2 c.	3/8 c.	1/4 c.
Honey	1 T.	2 t.	1 1/2 t.
Lecithin	1 1/2 t.	1 t.	3/4 t.
Oil	1/2 t.	1/4 t.	1/4 t.
Salt	1 1/2 t.	1 1/8 t.	3/4 t.
Instant Yeast	2 t.	1 1/2 t.	1 t.

Measure ingredients in order given. Select the white bread setting (or wheat bread if you have that option), then push the start button.

ONION-DILL BREAD

(Tastes like rye bread!)

	Large	Medium	Small
Lukewarm Water	1 1/2 c.	1 c.	2/3 c.
Sugar	4 T.	3 T.	2 T.
Dried Onion	2 T.	1 1/2 T.	1 T.
or Chopped Onion	1/2 c.	1/3 c.	1/4 c.
Salt	1 1/2 t.	1 t.	3/4 t.
Egg	1	1	1
Butter	1 T.	2 t.	1 1/2 t.
Instant Pwdrd Milk	1/2 c.	1/3 c.	1/4 c.
Dill Seed	4 t.	3 t.	2 t.
Wheat Flour	3 c.	2 1/4 c.	1 1/2 c.
Gluten Flour	4 T.	3 T.	2 T.
Instant Yeast	2 1/2 t.	2 t.	1 1/4 t.
Poppy Seeds	1 1/2 t.	1 t.	3/4 t.
Rye Flour	1 c.	3/4 c.	1/2 c.

Measure liquid ingredients into the breadmaker, followed by the dry ingredients. Add the yeast last. Program the breadmaker for basic white bread (or wheat bread if you have the option). Use the light crust setting, then begin the cycle.

ONION SOUP BREAD

	Large	Medium	Small
Instant Yeast	2 t.	1 1/2 t.	1 t.
Wheat Flour	3 1/4 c.	2 1/2 c.	1 5/8 c.
Gluten Flour	2 T.	1 1/2 T.	1 T.
Baking Soda	1/4 t.	3/8 t.	1/2 t.
Egg	1	1	1
Cottage Cheese	3/4 c.	1/2 c.	3/8 c.
Sour Cream	3/4 c.	1/2 c.	3/8 c.
Sugar	3 T.	2 1/4 T.	1 1/2 T.
Oil	1 1/2 T.	1 T.	2 t.
Water	1/4 c.	3 T.	2 T.
Lipton's™ Onion Soup Mix (dry)	3/4 env.	1/2 env.	3/8 env.

Place the first 5 ingredients into the breadmaker. slightly warm the next 6 ingredients and pour into the breadmaker. Select the wheat bread setting (or white if you have no wheat bread option), then start the machine.

Orange Bread

	Large	Medium	Small
Lukewarm Water	1/2 c.	1/3 c.	1/4 c.
Orange Juice	1 1/3 c.	1 c.	2/3 c.
Sugar	1/4 c.	3 T.	2 T.
Salt	1 1/2 t.	1 t.	3/4 t.
Butter	2 T.	1 1/2 T.	1 T.
Wheat Flour	4 c.	3 c.	2 c.
Grated Orange Peel	2 T.	1 1/2 T.	1 T.
Gluten Flour	3 1/2 T.	2 1/2 T.	1 3/4 T.
Instant Yeast	2 1/2 t.	1 3/4 t.	1 1/4 t.

Measure liquid ingredients into breadmaker. Add dry ingredients, ending with yeast and gluten flour.

Program the machine for white bread (or wheat bread if you have that option). After bread has baked and cooled, it is delicious when spread with a mixture of equal parts cream cheese and honey.

Peanut Bread

	Large	Medium	Small
Warm Water	1 c.	3/4 c.	1/2 c.
Egg	1	1	1
Butter	2 T.	1 1/2 T.	1 T.
Sugar	3 T.	2 1/4 T.	1 1/2 T.
Salt	1/2 t.	3/8 t.	1/4 t.
Wheat Flour	2 7/8 c.	2 1/4 c.	1 1/2 c.
Salted Peanuts	3/4 c.	1/2 c.	3/8 c.
Dry Milk	1/3 c.	4 T.	3 T.
Gluten Flour	2 T.	1 1/2 T.	1 T.
Instant Yeast	2 t.	1 1/2 t.	1 t.

Add all ingredients to the breadmaker in the order given. Select the wheat bread setting (or the white bread setting if you have no wheat bread option), then start the machine. When the bread is done, serve with your favorite jam or honey.

PEANUT BUTTER BREAD

	Large	Medium	Small
Lukewarm Water	1 1/2 c.	1 1/8 c.	3/4 c.
Wheat Flour	3 3/4 c.	2 7/8 c.	2 c.
Gluten Flour	3 T.	2 1/4 T.	1 1/2 T.
Salt	1 1/2 t.	1 t.	3/4 t.
Brown Sugar	1/2 c.	3/8 c.	1/4 c.
Peanut Butter (chunky)	3/4 c.	1/2 c.	3/8 c.
Yeast	2 t.	1 1/2 t.	1 t.

Add ingredients to breadmaker in order given. Make sure peanut butter is at room temperature. Start the breadmaker on the white bread setting (or wheat bread if you have that option).

PECAN-DATE BREAD

	Large	Medium	Small
Yeast	2 t.	1 1/2 t.	1 t.
Lukewarm Water	1 1/2 c.	1 c.	3/4 c.
Butter	2 T.	1 1/2 T.	1 T.
Wheat Flour	3 1/4 c.	2 3/8 c.	1 3/4 c.
Gluten Flour	3 T.	2 1/4 T.	1 1/2 T.
Dry Milk	2 T.	1 1/2 T.	1 T.
Salt	1 1/2 t.	1 1/8 t.	3/4 t.
Honey	2 T.	1 1/2 T.	1 T.
Chopped Dates	1/2 c.	3/8 c.	1/4 c.
Chopped Pecans	3 T.	2 T.	1 1/2 T.

Add all the ingredients to the breadmaker in the order given. Select the wheat bread setting (or white bread if you have no wheat bread selection), then start the cycle.

PECAN AND ONION BREAD
(Surprisingly Good!)

	Large	Medium	Small
Yeast	2 t.	1 1/2 t.	1/2 t.
Warm Milk	1 1/8 c.	3/4 c.	1/2 c.
Butter	1/4 c.	3 T.	2 T.
Sugar	1 1/2 t.	1 t.	3/4 t.
Salt 1 1/2 t.	1 1/8 t.	3/4 t.	
Wheat Flour	3 c.	2 1/4 c.	1 1/2 c.
Gluten Flour	2 T.	1 1/2 T.	1 T.

Red Onion (chopped)	1/2 c.	3/8 c.	1/4 c.
Pecans (chopped)	3/4 c.	1/2 c.	3/8 c.

Add all ingredients to the breadmaker in the order given. Select the wheat bread setting (or white if you have no wheat bread option), then start the machine.

PEPPER SPICE BREAD

	Large	Medium	Small
Yeast	2 t.	1 1/2 t.	1 t.
Very Warm Water	3/4 c.	1/2 c.	3/8 c.
Corn Syrup	2 T.	1 1/2 T.	1 T.
Honey	2 T.	1 1/2 T.	1 T.
Egg	1	1	1
Butter	1/4 c.	3 T.	2 T.
Sugar	1/4 c.	3 T.	2 T.
Dry Milk	1/4 c.	3 T.	2 T.
Salt 1/2 t.	3/8 t.	1/4 t.	
Wheat Flour	2 7/8 c.	2 1/4 c.	1 1/2 c.
Gluten Flour	2 T.	1 1/2 T.	1 T.
Pecans (chopped)	1/4 c.	3 T.	2 T.

Black Pepper	1/2 t.	1/3 t.	1/4 t.
Whole Anise Seed	1 t.	3/4 t.	1/2 t.
Cinnamon	1/4 t.	1/4 t.	1/8 t.
Allspice	1/4 t.	1/8 t.	1/8 t.

Add all ingredients to breadmaker in the order given. Select the wheat bread (or the white bread setting if you have no wheat bread option on your machine), then start the machine. This bread is rich and spicy, and is a delicious complement to any mild soup or stew.

PRUNE BREAD

	Large	Medium	Small
Warm Water	1 1/4 c.	1 c.	5/8 c.
Pitted Prunes(quartered)	1 c.	3/4 c.	1/2 c.
Butter	1 T.	3/4 T.	1/2 T.
Brown Sugar	3 T.	2 1/4 T.	1 1/2 T.
Salt 1 t.	3/4 t.	1/2 t.	
Wheat Flour	2 7/8 c.	2 1/4 c.	1 1/2 c.
Gluten Flour	2 T.	1 1/2 T.	1 T.
Instant Yeast	2 t.	1 1/2 t.	1 t.

Add all the ingredients to your Breadmaker in the order given. Select the wheat bread setting if you have that option, otherwise use white.

PUMPERNICKEL BREAD

	Large	Medium	Small
Warm Water	1 1/4 c.	1 c.	5/8 c.
Oil	1 T.	3/4 T.	1/2 T.
Molasses	3 T.	2 1/4 T.	1 1/2 T.
Cocoa	1 T.	2 1/4 t.	1 1/2 t.
Salt	1 1/2 t.	1 1/8 t.	3/4 t.
Caraway Seed	2 t.	1 1/2 t.	1 t.
Wheat Flour	3 c.	2 1/4 c.	1 1/2c.
Gluten Flour	3 T.	2 1/4 T.	1 1/2 T.
Rye Flour	5/8 c.	1/2 c.	3/8 c.
Instant Yeast	3 t.	2 1/4 t.	1 1/2 t.

Add all ingredients to the breadmaker in the order given. Select the wheat bread setting (or the white bread setting if you have no wheat bread option). Use the light crust setting, as this bread will be very dark. It will also be quite heavy, but the flavor will be superb!

PUMPKIN BREAD

	Large	Medium	Small
Lukewarm Water	1 1/3 c.	1 c.	2/3 c.
Pumpkin	2/3 c.	1/2 c.	1/3 c.
Oil	2 T.	1 1/2 T.	1 T.
Brown Sugar	1/3 c.	3 T.	1 1/2 T.
Salt	2 t.	1 1/2 t.	1 t.
Cinnamon	1 1/2 t.	1 1/8 t.	3/4 t.
Cloves	1/2 t.	1/3 t.	1/4 t.
Nutmeg	1/2 t.	1/3 t.	1/4 t.
Ginger	1/2 t.	1/3 t.	1/4 t.
Wheat Flour	3 1/2 c.	2 3/4 c.	1 7/8 c.
Gluten Flour	3 T.	2 1/4 T.	1 1/2 T.
Instant Yeast	1 T.	2 1/4 t.	1 1/2 t.

Measure all ingredients into breadmaker in the order given. Program the breadmaker for basic bread (or whole wheat bread if your machine has that option). Since the pumpkin, spices, and wheat flour create a very dark bread, be sure to use the light crust setting. This bread is very good as toast for breakfast.

RAISIN BRAN BREAD

	Large	Medium	Small
Warm Water	1 c.	3/4 c.	1/2 c.
Lecithin	1 1/2 t.	1 t.	3/4 t.
Oil	1/2 t.	1/4 t.	1/4 t.
Brown Sugar	4 T.	3 T.	2 T.
Salt	1/2 t.	1/3 t.	1/4 t.
Wheat Flour	1 7/8 c.	1 3/8 c.	7/8 c.
Raisin Bran Cereal	1 1/2 c.	1 1/8 c.	3/4 c.
Baking Soda	1/4 t.	1/8 t.	1/8 t.
Gluten Flour	1 1/2 T.	1 1/8 T.	3/4 T.
Instant Yeast	1 1/2 t.	1 t.	3/4 t.

Measure all ingredients into breadmaker in order listed. Select wheat bread (or white if you have no wheat bread option), then start the machine. This bread may not rise very high, but it is a very nutritious and tasty bread.

RAISIN CINNAMON BREAD

	Large	Medium	Small
Lukewarm Water	1 1/3 c.	1 c.	2/3 c.
Wheat Flour	3 1/2 c.	2 3/4 c.	1 3/4 c.
Instant Yeast	2 1/2 t.	2 t.	1 1/4 t.
Instant Dry Milk	1/2 c.	1/3 c.	1/4 c.
Cinnamon	1 1/2 t.	1 t.	3/4 t.
Sugar	1/3 c.	4 T.	2 1/2 T.
Salt	1 1/2 t.	1 1/8 t.	3/4 t.
Butter	2 T.	1 1/2 T.	1 T.
Gluten Flour	2 T.	1 1/2 T.	1 T.

Measure warm water into the breadmaker, followed by the other ingredients, adding yeast and gluten flour last. Program your breadmaker for raisin bread. After dough is mixed together, make sure that the dough is the desired consistency, adding a little more flour or water as needed. When the machine beeps, (or is almost through the second kneading, if you don't have a raisin bread setting), add remaining ingredients.

Raisins	1 c.	3/4 c.	1/2 c.
Chopped Nuts	1/2 c.	3/8 c.	1/4 c.

SIX-GRAIN BREAD

	Large	Medium	Small
Lukewarm Water	1 1/2 c.	1 1/8 c.	3/4 c.
Wheat Flour	3 1/4 c.	2 1/2 c.	1 5/8 c.
Instant Yeast	1 1/2 t.	1 1/8 t.	3/4 t.
Whey or Dry Milk	2 T.	1 1/2 T.	1 T.
Lecithin	2 T.	1 1/2 T.	1 T.
Six-Grain Cereal	1/4 c.	3 T.	2 T.
Salt	1 1/2 t.	1 1/8 t.	3/4 t.
Honey or Molasses	2 T.	1 1/2 T.	1 T.
Gluten Flour	3 T.	2 1/4 T.	4 t.

Measure water into breadmaker. Add rest of ingredients, with yeast being last. Program the breadmaker for basic white bread (or wheat bread if you have that option), then start the cycle.

SOUTH OF THE BORDER BREAD

	Large	Medium	Small
Warm Water	1 1/4 c.	1 c.	5/8 c.
Egg	1	1	1
Sugar	2 t.	1 1/2 t.	1 t.
Lecithin	1 T.	3/4 T.	1/2 T.
Salt	1/2 t.	3/8 t.	1/4 t.
Cheese (shredded)	1/2 c.	3/8 c.	1/4 c.
Chilies	1 T.	3/4 T.	1/2 T.
Corn	1/2 c.	3/8 c.	1/4 c.
Cornmeal	3/4 c.	5/8 c.	1/2 c.
Wheat Flour	2 7/8 c.	2 1/4 c.	1 1/2 c.
Gluten Flour	2 T.	1 1/2 T.	1 T.
Instant Yeast	2 t.	1 1/2 t.	1 t.

Drain corn, if it is in liquid. Chop the chilies if they are whole. Add ingredients to the breadmaker in the order given. Select the white or wheat bread setting, depending on which machine you have, then start the machine. This bread is wonderful with any Mexican meal.

CHAPTER FOUR

CAUSES OF POOR QUALITY BREAD

If you are not pleased with your bread, or have noticed a particular problem with your bread, you may be able to find a quick and easy solution in this chapter.

The problems and solutions in the first section relate to making bread by hand or by breadmixer, where the bread has to bake in an oven.

The second section refers to difficulties occurring only with automatic breadmakers.

An asterisk(*) will mark problems and solutions that are common to bread made by any of these methods.

HAND-MADE AND BREADMIXER BREAD

1. Does your finished bread have a poor shape?

You may have left some air bubbles in your dough before the last rise in the pan. Also, there may have been uneven heat distribution in the oven. Make sure that your loaves have enough space between them while baking for air and heat to circulate evenly between the loaves.

*2. Is your bread crumbly, with poor volume?**

Your flour may have been too coarsely milled, the wheat could have been low in protein, or the dough may not have been kneaded long enough. Any of these factors would have kept the gluten from developing enough to bind the bread together. The result is crumbly bread. If too much oil or fat was added to the dough, it would have over-tenderized the bread, causing it to crumble also. The bread may have been baked before it had risen sufficiently, or the oven temperature may have been too low. In an oven that is too cool, the loaves will not set quickly enough. They continue to rise until the cell walls collapse. When the bread finally does bake, the loaves are flat and crumbly.

3. Does your bread hang over the side of the pan on one or both sides?

Your dough may have been too soft. Use a little more flour next time. The dough may have been allowed to rise too long (more than double), or there may have been too much dough in the pan to begin with (it takes three cups of dough for a standard pan). Finally, if the oven was too cool, or if the heat was not able to distribute evenly (if your pans were too close together in the oven), the bread may have fallen the side of the pan where the heat was the lowest.

4. Is there a crack along one, or both sides of your loaf after baking?

Uneven heat circulation in the oven could have caused the cracks. Make sure that pans are far enough apart to allow heat and air circulation while the bread is baking. Dough that is too dry can also crack during baking. Use a little less flour next time.

5. Are there air bubbles under the top crust after baking?

Mold your loaves in such a way that the air bubbles are worked out before the loaves are placed in the pans. Also, be sure that your bread doesn't rise too high before baking. Finally, the oven has to be hot enough to set the yeast cells in the dough immediately, or the bread will rise too high in the oven before it bakes, creating an air bubble under the crust.

6. Do deep cracks appear in the sides or top of your loaves after baking?

Usually, deep cracks are caused by dough that has not been kneaded long enough, and the gluten has not developed. The bread just won't hold together, and it cracks as it bakes.

7. Does your bread have an abnormally thick crust that is hard to chew?

You may not have kneaded the bread long enough. The gluten won't hold the bread together, making the finished product heavy and crusty. If the rising period was too long, the dough may have collapsed, also causing a thick, heavy loaf and crust. An oven that was too cool would have the same effect; it would allow the bread to continue rising in the oven until it collapsed. The loaf would be heavy and the crust would be thick.

*8. Are the cell walls inside your sliced bread big and thick instead of small and delicate?**

If your flour has not been milled fine enough, the bread will be coarse and heavy. If the dough has not been kneaded enough, the gluten will not develop properly, and again, the cell walls will be thick and large. If the dough has not been allowed to rise enough, the cell walls inside the bread will be compact, and will appear thick and heavy.

9. Are there streaks in your finished loaves?*

Streaks are caused by adding flour after you are already through kneading the dough. It doesn't get a chance to incorporate into the dough, and it forms streaks. Oil or fat on your hands while you mold dough into loaves can also cause streaks. Use a little less oil next time.

10. Are your loaves dense and thick at the bottom, but crumbly at the top?

If loaves are placed on a surface that is too cool during rising, it will prevent the loaf from rising uniformly. The top of the loaf will rise, but the bottom will stay compact. If your oven is too cool during baking, the loaves will continue to rise too long in the oven before the outside crust becomes hard enough to prevent any more rising.

11. Are your loaves coarse in texture?*

Poorly milled wheat, as well as insufficient kneading will prevent the proper development of gluten. The texture of your finished bread will be coarse and heavy. If dough is not allowed to rise long enough, or if it is too cool to rise, it will also be compact and coarse. Finally, if the dough rises too long, and collapses, the finished bread will be heavy and the texture will be very coarse.

AUTOMATIC BREADMAKER BREAD

1. Is your loaf compact and heavy without enough rise?

Your wheat may be milled too coarsely, preventing gluten from being able to develop. Your flour may be too low in protein. Make sure that you have enough gluten flour in the dough. Your yeast may be old. There may have been insufficient rise time, or there may have been too much flour added in the recipe, making the dough too heavy.

2. Does your loaf rise and then collapse before baking?

There may be too much liquid in the recipe. Add a little more flour next time. The rise time may have been too long, or the recipe may be too large for the pan. Lower the temperature of the ingredients; they may be too warm.

3. Does your loaf rise so high that it is crumbly at the top?

You may need more salt in the recipe, or you may need less yeast and sugar. Dough may be a little too light; add a little more flour next time.

4. Does your bread taste yeasty?

Use less yeast, less sugar, or both.

5. Is the top of your loaf bulgy and cracked?

Dough is too dry and doesn't form well. Use less flour next time.

CONCLUSION

Regardless of what type of mill you use, or what type of bread mixer you have-or if you don't have one at all-you can incorporate whole-grain or whole wheat bread into your diet. With good wheat, a good mill, and a willingness to try something new (or old), you can find good health and much satisfaction in learning the principles of good breadmaking with whole wheat flour.

I wish you success in your whole wheat bread-making endeavors.

ACKNOWLEDGMENTS

There are many people who have contributed to the writing of this book. I owe them all many thanks. My sincere appreciation goes to:

Dr. John Hal Johnson, Dept. of Food Science and Nutrition at Brigham Young University in Provo, Utah, who answered many of my questions about breadmaking.

Dr. Gur S. Ranhotra, Cereal Chemist and Director of Nutrition Research for the American Institute of Baking in Manhattan, Kansas, who shared valuable nutrition information with me.

Maura Bean of the Cereals Group at the USDA Western Regional Laboratory in Berkeley, California, who also answered many questions for me on the process of breadmaking.

Mr. Sherman Robinson and his staff at Lehi Roller Mills, Incorporated, in Lehi, Utah, who shared valuable information on wheat and whole wheat flour.

Mr. Dick Sperry and Mr. Tom Dickson of Kitchen Technologies in Lindon, Utah, whose knowledge of whole wheat breadmaking have been very helpful.

Mr. Don Norton of the English Department of Brigham Young University in Provo, Utah, for his editing and encouragement.

The Zojirushi America Corporation, The Hitachi Home Electronics Company, and Back to Basics of Sandy, Utah, with the Panasonic Auto Bakery, all of whom allowed me the use of their machines as I learned about automatic breadmakers.

Jil Abegg for the health and nutrition tips in *How to Save Big Money Grocery and Household Shopping.*

LeArta Moulton and Rita Bingham for the breadmaking tips contained in *The Quick, Wholesome Foods Video.*

Rita Bingham for her ideas on milling beans, contained in her book, *Rita's Beans.*

I am most grateful to my husband, Larry, and my family, for their help and patience, as we made many batches of bread, then took the time to write the story of all that bread.

ABOUT THE AUTHOR

Diana Ballard has experimented with whole wheat breadmaking for the last 24 years. Because of the challenges of whole wheat breadmaking, she has spent many hours searching for answers to questions about the process. Unfortunately, she has found many recipes, but very little information about the methods and concepts involved.

After thoroughly researching whole wheat breadmaking, Diana has written this book to share the secrets known by professional bakers, cereal chemists, and educators.

Diana is married to Larry L. Ballard and lives in Salem, Utah. She and her husband are the parents of five children, all of whom have many memories of hot wheat bread from Mama's kitchen.

PERSONAL NOTES AND RECIPES

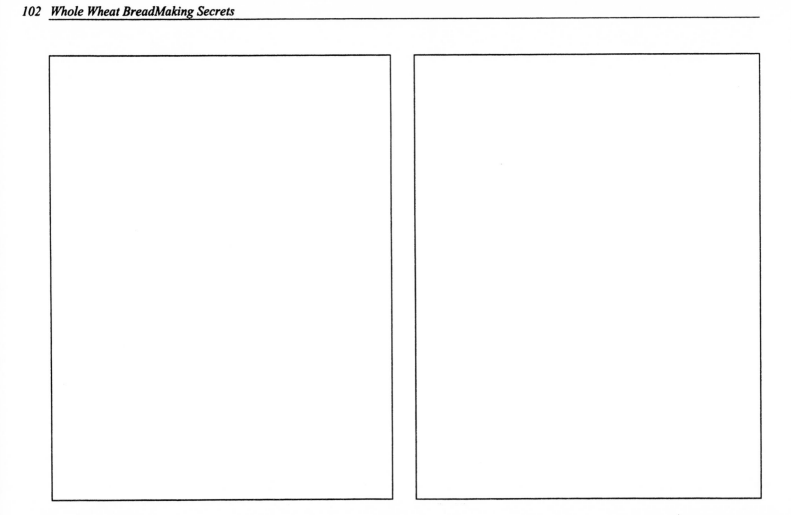

FOOTNOTES

[1] Most commercial stone grinding mills now use hard granite stones to mill wheat.

[2] "Contribution of Wheat to Human Nutrition." Gur Ranhotra, Ph.D. Director, Nutrition Research, American Institute of Baking, Research Dept. Technical Bulletin, Vol. XIV, Issue 2, February, 1992.
"Wheat and Bread: Available Nutrients and Dietary Role." Gur Ranhotra, Ph.D. and Ann Bock, R.D., American Institute of Baking, Research Dept. Technical Bulletin, Vol. IV, Issue 5, May, 1982.
"Wheat Flour Milling." Dale Eustace, Ph.D., Department of Grain Science and Industry, Kansas State University, Manhattan, Kansas. Research Dept. Technical Bulletin, Vol. X, Issue 11, November, 1988.
"Wheat: Chemistry and Technology." Vol. I, p. 133. Y. Pomeranz (editor), 1988. American Association of Cereal Chemists, St. Paul, Minn.

[3] "Nutritive Value of Foods" USDA Home Garden Bulletin No. 72, 1981.

[4] "Wheat and Bread: Available Nutrients and Dietary Role." Gur Ranhotra, Ph.D. and Ann Bock, R.D., American Institute of Baking, Research Dept. Technical Bulletin, Vol. IV, Issue 5, May, 1982.

[5] "Yeast Fermentation in Bread Making." Research Dept. Technical Bulletin, Vol. V, Issue 12, December, 1983. Gary W. Sanderson, Gerald Reed, Bernard Bruinsma, and Elmer J. Cooper, Universal Foods Corporation, Milwaukee, Wisconsin.